The serious
book of
One-liners

The serious book of One-liners

George Coote

Gap Publishing

THE SERIOUS BOOK OF ONE-LINERS
© G. COOTE 1997

Published in 1997 by
GAP PUBLISHING
44 Wendell St, Norman Park
Queensland 4170, Australia

Reprinted 1998 (twice)

Typesetting by Ads-Up Graphics Pty Ltd
Cover design by Concept Australia Corporate Design Group
Cover art and cartoons by Daniel Boermans

Printed in Australia by
McPherson's Printing Group

ISBN 0 947163 30 1

GEORGE COOTE has been a Melbourne-based journalist for forty years, most of this time as a travel writer. He is a life member of the Australian Society of Travel Writers.

Over the past five years George has written The Serious Joke Book series, over 50,000 jokes classified under 300 headings. The original aim was to create a reference work for journalists and copywriters who wished to spice up their work with the appropriate humourous twist. However the public embraced the idea and the first two titles sold over 100,000 copies each in Australia, New Zealand and the United Kingdom.

Although using the same formula of indexing for quick retrieval, this volume of one-liners is different. The jokes are easier to find and to remember and will prove invaluable for speakers, writers and raconteurs.

Contents

THE contents have been assembled into categories which are common to us all and can be quickly retrieved for delivery from either the rostrum or the public bar.

We all relate to families, politics, health, religion, sex and the professions while one-line throwaways on the all-embracing topics of the weather, statistics or amazing facts can liven any discussion.

Introduction

A good journalist is like a dead wombat, always with an ear to the ground. He is usually armed with a pen and notebook, which is how these one-liners were collected.

The aim of this book is to supply speakers, writers and raconteurs with an armory of over 3000 wise-cracks which are readily retrievable for the right occasion. They range from being serious, refined, humourous to downright rude. Use them according to the company you're currently keeping.

Why one-liners?

Words are the means by which we confuse each other, so the less used the better. In fact, if it goes without saying, let it.

Timely one-liners can pack more wallop with their economy of words than volumes of diatribe which can smother the point. It's the same with a joke which, if told well, needs construction, timing, a punchline and a good memory, while the one-liner is easily handled.

While primarily slanted towards the public speaker this volume can be a source of pleasure to all who love the richness of the English language, its double entendres, malapropisms, mispronunciations and linguistic cock-ups.

Repartee means being armed with a ready and witty reply. Repartee is a street-fighter insult with a dress suit on.

This book will provide those prompt rejoinders that will demolish your antagonist with piercing accuracy, eruidite wit and spontaneity. A tad better than telling him to "get stuffed".

The advantage of the one-liner is that it doesn't have to be related to the text of your speech or fit the conversation. Unlike a joke which needs to be memorised, constructed and delivered with timing to the punchline, the one-liner becomes the pot shot which can be fired off at any time and can hardly be messed up.

Public speaking

Given a free choice most people would rather be amused than be on the receiving end of a lecture, and no matter how informative the speech might be it will be improved with a sprinkling of one-liners selected to emphasise a point.

For most people, public speaking is a fate worse than death, but it doesn't have to be. If you are well armed, it's a doddle. Public speaking is a feat of mind over mutter.

Use this book to select the one-liners which tickle your fancy. Jot down the key words on the back of several business cards and shuffle them forward in your hand whenever a mental block appears to be on the way.

Notes are essential unless you are a radio announcer, a politician or have a natural gift of the gab.

Let's face it, you have been asked to speak because you are credited with knowing what you are talking about, so pre-write your speech to ensure that the message is understood.

Even using a written speech can be spoofed to advantage. When you step up to the lectern reach into your inside pocket and produce a note and start reading: "A loaf of bread, milk and butter. And if you come home pissed again tonight you can sleep on your own....oops. Sorry, wrong note." (Look miffed about halfway through this note as you realise it is the wrong one).

Put it back and fumble for the real thing.

Your arsenal of one-liners can be written on the back of business cards you exchanged at the cocktail session before the speech. Saves using your own cards.

Shuffle them to your priority and refer to them whenever your serious address could do with a lift.

1
Public Speaking

Let me introduce ...

THE MC is the bloke who introduces people who need no introduction. If you find yourself in this position then here are a few ploys for presenting your speaker. "Now let me introduce ..."

I AM not going to bore you with a lot of old jokes, so I will now introduce you to a man who can do that much better than I can.

OUR next speaker is a man who is constantly sought. Tonight, for instance, we had to search three pubs and a wine bar.

AT this juncture in procedings we usually introduce a man of unusual talent, eloquence and wit. Tonight, we depart from that tradition.

IF you were listening last week you will have noticed our deliberate mistake. And here he is again.

NOW let me introduce a man who started life as a handicapped, impoverished, and insecure street sweeper in Gloomstown, and who, unfortunately, never lived up to his early promise.

HE is a man who is going places. And frankly, the sooner the better.

OUR next speaker is working under a handicap tonight. He is sober.

OUR next speaker needs no introduction. He hasn't turned up.

SOME people bring happiness wherever they go. Our next speaker brings happiness "whenever" he goes.

AS soon as this man is introduced the evening will pick up speed. Which is what always happens when a show starts to go downhill.

OUR speaker tonight is here under embarrassing circumstances. Nobody invited him.

IT'S been said of our next speaker that he is the wittiest man in the country. And here's the man who said it.

MUCH has been written and said about our next guest, and here he is tonight, in a bid to deny it.

UNFORTUNATELY I have to announce two disappointments tonight. The Prime Minister couldn't make it, but our next speaker has.

SO many people start with the words, "I am not really a speech-maker." Then they spend the next half hour proving it.

HE'S not the right person to make a speech. Last time he managed to screw up the Minute's Silence.

THANK you for such a flattering introduction. It makes me wish I had prepared something important to say.

THESE are not my figures I'm quoting. These facts are from someone who knows what he's talking about.

EVERY rose has its thorn
    That's the catch life teaches
    There hasn't been a free lunch yet
    Without those boring speeches.

TONIGHT, it is my task to speak to you, and your task to listen. I just hope we finish at the same time.

I SEE some of you have heard me before and come early to get the best seats — near the door.

(AS an aside). I have noticed an odd coincidence. There are 500 of us here tonight and we have all ordered the same meal.

ALL the money raised tonight will go towards charity. It may not actually get there, but it will be going towards it.

I WILL conclude now as there is only five minutes left and I like to leave time for applause.

FINALLY, I wish to thank this audience for their fine support, and I will wear it all times.

To hecklers

WOULD you like to step outside and say that?
  Good. Well I'll stay here and finish my speech.

DON'T move. I want to forget you exactly the way you are.

IF they ever put a price on your head, take it.

LISTEN. When I want your opinion I'll give it to you.

I HAVE listened to your humble opinion and it certainly is.

Speakers

PUBLIC speakers should be light, tight, bright and right.

THERE are many who believe an orator is an unpopular wind instrument.

IF people listened to themselves more often they would talk less.

THREE rules for speakers: Stand up. Speak up. Shut up.

WE stand up to be seen, speak up to be heard and shut up to be appreciated.

YOU can't out-talk a man who knows what he is talking about.

THE man who rises to the occasion should also know when to sit down.

THERE is no point in speaking unless you can improve on silence.

THE after-dinner speaker either drives his message home to his audience or drives his audience home.

THE best conversationalist is the bloke who lets others do the talking.

THE person who says the art of conversation is dead has never waited outside a public phone box.

THE best after-dinner speech is: "Waiter, bring me both bills."

THE best way to stay awake during an after-dinner speech is to give it.

THE speaker asked the MC if had put enough fire into the speech. "Better if you had put more speech into the fire," he replied.

Roasts

WHAT can we say about our guest of honour? There are some things that go without saying. Unfortunately he isn't one of them.

OF course, there is a lot to be said in his favour, but it's not half as interesting as the shit I've dug up to tell you tonight.

SUCCESS hasn't changed him. He is still the mean bastard he always was.

THIS man is an inspiration to us all. Let's face it, if he can make it then surely any dickhead can.

WHEN his family, friends and workmates heard we were to honour him in this way tonight their response was unanimous. To a man they demanded to know "Why?"

SINCE I met him a year ago there hasn't been a day when I haven't thought about him. And I haven't thought about him today either.
See *Insults*, page 145

Weather

EVERYBODY talks about the weather so it is natural to make the subject your opening gambit. As Bob Dylan said: "You don't need to be a weatherman to know which way the wind blows." If you don't think the topic important, then consider, the number of people at your funeral will depend on the weather.

IT was so cold coming to the hall tonight that I saw the local flasher describing himself to a group of women in the park.

IT was as cold as a barmaid's heart.

ONCE I discovered a town so cold that all the inhabitants lived somewhere else.

IT was so cold on the Antarctic expedition that when he returned his fiancée broke it off.

IT was so cold it could freeze the walls off a bark humpy.

MY room is so cold that every time I open the door the light goes on.

IT was so cold the candle froze and we couldn't blow it out.

IT was so cold words came out of our mouths as chunks of ice and we had to fry them to see what we were talking about.

A MAN who saves for a rainy day gets a lot of bad weather reports from his relatives.

WEATHER forecasters are forthright. They manage to get one in four right.

IT has been so dry in the drought-stricken Outback town that the shire council closed two lanes of the municipal swimming pool.

IT has been so dry the frogs were taking swimming lessons.

IT was as dry as a Pommie's towel.

BECAUSE of the severe drought there is to be a rain-making ceremony next Sunday. It will be held in Central Park, or if wet, in the town hall.

THE wind blew so hard...
   it blew three dogs off their chains...
   a chook facing east laid the same egg three times ...
   it blew the pricks off a barbed wire fence.

IT'S an ill-wind that blows when you leave the hair-dresser.

I asked Monty how he found the weather in Tasmania.
   He said he just opened the door and there it was.

THE Bureau predicts a pleasant 48 degrees tomorrow:
10 in the morning 25 at noon and 13 in the evening.

MY uncle worked in the Weather Bureau for years,
but when he was promoted to the Canberra office he
only lasted a month. The weather didn't agree with
him.

HE went to Mexico where the weather was more
predictable: Chili today, hot tamale.

THE BBC announcer said: Today it will be muggy,
followed by Tuggy, Weggy, Thurggy and Fruggy.

WHEN the floods came the maestro floated by on a
double bass, and his wife accompanied him on the
piano.

IT was cold as the depths of a polar bear's pool,
and as cold as the tip of an Icelander's tool.

AND for the philosophical: The good seaman
weathers the storm he cannot avoid, and avoids the
storm he cannot weather.

Last time I spoke here

A COMMENT on the last time you spoke here implies you've done it all before and that you're full of confidence.

THE last time I spoke here I asked if those in the back row could hear me and a bloke stood to say he could ... and that he would gladly change places with anybody who couldn't.

THE last function here was the World Churches' Conference on family planning. Unfortunately the Vatican's representative had to pull out at the last minute.

THE last time I attended this hall was for a conference on premature ejaculation. Although I got here five minutes early the meeting was over.

THE last time I spoke here I was to address the annual convention of the Clairvoyant Society, but it was cancelled due to unforseen circumstances.

LAST time I spoke in this hall a female streaker dashed down the aisle. Fortunately, she was caught by the bouncers.

BY the way, the food is so bad in this place the mice send out for take-away.

THE last time I spoke here was at the National Conference of Henpecked Husbands. Nobody arrived. The members weren't allowed out.

WE are only here tonight due to a late cancellation by the National Apathetic Society, due to lack of interest.

THEN there was the incident when the Claustrophobia Society's convention was held here. Only one member turned up and and kept screaming "Let me out!"

I SPOKE here last time because the Hernia Society needed my support.

THE last time I delivered this speech was to the inmates of the State Prison, and I apologise to those who have heard it before.

Tough times

YOUR listeners will always appreciate a few biographical details so they can get to know you.It doesn't matter if your real life has been boring. They don't want to hear that. Cobble together as many of the following one liners you are comfortable with and tell your fans about the tough old days.

A STRING of one liners unashamedly woven into a yarn on a single topic is the easiest way to hold your listeners and can be dropped at any time you want to revert back to your serious address.

There is no plot, construction or punchline to worry about, just one-word prompts.

While they are short and punchy in themselves, they have far more effect when queued up in the same story. Sure, it requires a good memory and a little practice for delivery, but with a prompt card in your hand ready for the occasional glance to find the key word, the story line should flow with each one-liner bolstering the next.

One of the easiest forms of monologue is your own "biography". We all find it easy to talk about ourselves, so it is comparatively simple to deliver your own preposterous life story around a dinner table of strangers or friends, or even from the rostrum.

Here's an example, but remember it is an overloaded version. And it can be readily released at the drop of several trigger questions which are bound to crop up in such groups; like what do you do for a living, how long have you lived in these parts, or where do you come from?

Where do I come from?

Actually, I am part Irish and part Italian. (If you have their attention with this line, follow with): I'm Irish by my mother's side, and Italian by a friend of my father's!

THE family was in iron and steel. My mother ironed and my father stole. (Now ramble on)

I WAS born at an early age. Premature actually. I am a man before my time. I am really only 25.

IF my father hadn't been so shy and retiring I would have been three years older than I am now.

MY birth was a surprise to my Mum... and everyone else in the Tankerville Arms at the time.

I WAS an unwanted child. My father spent weeks trying to find a loophole in my birth certificate.

WHEN I was born he tried to collect on his accident insurance.

MY mother was a little disappointed. She had wanted a girl. But she said later that at least a boy was her second choice.

I WAS abandoned on a doorstep. I wasn't found there, because the door opened out.
   I was found two somersaults out on the roadway.

THERE was a note pinned to my shawl.
 It read: "Keep your head down. The door opens out. Mum!"

WE were so poor the woman next door had my brother.

HE was a Caesarean birth. It didn't affect him, but I noticed he always left the house through the front window.

WE were so poor we thought cutlery was jewellery.

POOR! We were so poor burglars used to break in and leave things.

WHEN I was a tiny tot my Dad used to play games with me. He used to throw me in the air, then walk away.

ONE day he took me aside and left me there.

HE was tough on us. He made us run two miles every night. By the end of the week we were 14 miles from home.

HIS swimming training was tougher. He threw us off the deep end of the pier. Swimming to shore wasn't so bad. Getting out of the bag was the hard part.

ONCE, in a kind gesture, Dad said he would take us to the zoo. Mum said, "No way. If they want them let them come and get them."

A CHARITY worker knocked on the door and said he was collecting for the Children's Home. Dad gave him three of us.

EVERY meal time Dad used to feed us with whip and a chair.

MY mother went to the clinic to seek an abortion. They said it was too late. I was already in Grade Three.

MY parents hated me so much they hired the kid next door as a stand-in for our home movies.

WHEN I asked for music lessons they gave me a drum and told me to beat it.

I HAD acne so bad my dog used to call me Spot.

WHEN the wolf came to our door he used to bring his own sandwiches.

THE wolf was at the door so often we called him Rex.

OUR school was the only one which still retained capital punishment.

THE kids at our school were so tough the teacher used to play hookey.

WHEN we went to school my Dad used to paint the house a different colour and change the number on the front gate.

OUR Mum used to wrap our lunch in a road map.

WE went to an immoral school. It had no principal and it had no class.

I WAS sent home with a note for my parents. They wanted a written excuse for my presence.

THE teacher asked me to name two pronouns.
    I said: "Who? Me?"

SHE asked: "What's three times three?"
    I said: "Nine."
    She said: "That's pretty good."
    I said it was bloody perfect.

SHE said my essay was exactly word for word the same as my brother's.
    I said of course it was. It's about the same dog.

SHE asked which month had 28 days.
    I said they all had.

TOUGH? We used to have bread and pullet most nights and we all had racing colours on our knives and forks.

ON Saturday night Mum would make windmill pie.
(Here you pause and hope somebody asks: "What is windmill pie?")
You get a bit if it goes round!

OUR house was so messy that once some vandals broke in and did a hundred dollars' worth of improvement.

THE house was such a mess we used to wipe our feet before we went out.

OUR house was so dirty the flies chipped in and bought a fly-screen door.

The neighbourhood

OUR neighbourhood was so tough you could walk ten blocks without leaving the scene of the crime.

ANY kid in our street with two ears was a sissy.

ANY cat with a tail in our neighbourhood was a tourist.

WE used to call the nuns the Little Sisters of the Rich.

EVEN the muggers walked around in pairs.

ONCE a storm swept through our town and did $200,000 worth of improvement.

THE city fathers tried to link with a twin city abroad. The best they could do was to form a suicide pact with Sarejevo.

Proverbs to live by

IN this section we have the one-liner bullets which will prod your listeners to attention. Some are so profound they should be dropped into the middle of your address whether you have lost your place or not, in case the audience has drifted away. Simply look them straight in the eye and say with sincerity and conviction:

TIMING is the essential factor in the success of any rain dance.

NO woman has ever shot her husband while he was doing the dishes.

NOTHING succeeds like a toothless budgie.

IMAGINATION gallops while judgment goes on foot.

A SHALLOW thinker never leaves a deep impression.

ONLY the mediocre are always at their best.

REALITY is for people who can't cope with drugs.

WHAT the eye doesn't see the feet will fall over.

LOCKJAW means never having to say you're sorry.

SADO-masochism means never having to say you are sorry.

VASECTOMY means never having to say you're sorry.

WHEN you sling mud you are losing ground.

WHEN arguing with a fool, make sure he is not doing the same thing.

THE heaviest baggage for a traveller can be an empty purse.

AN optimist is one who thinks the future is uncertain.

A HAIR on the head is worth two on the brush.

NEVER judge a book by its movies.

IF at first you don't succeed, quit.

IF at first you do succeed, don't take any more chances.

WHEN you don't succeed after trying again, read the bloody instructions.

IF all you have is a hammer, everything looks like a nail.

YOU can lead a horse to water but you can't lead a whore to culture.

YOU can lead a horticulture but you cannot make her think.

THE scene may change, but only for the lead dog.

THIN yaks leave light tracks.

NO leg is too short to reach the ground.

A LEGLESS tramp is a low-down bum.

ONE-legged girls are a push-over.

THAT the pill can stop an unwanted pregnancy is a popular misconception.

CONTRACEPTIVES should be used on all conceivable occasions.

ARTIFICIAL insemination is so reliable because it lessens the chance of a cock-up.

TO err is human, but to really stuff things up requires a computer.

IF it wasn't for the last minute, nothing would get done.

IT is often the dead wood which holds up a tree, and just because it is still standing doesn't mean it's alive.

TWO fat people will walk side by side whether they know each other or not.

HALF a loaf is better than no tea-break at all.

ONE door closes, another slams in your face.

PEOPLE who are resistant to change cannot resist change for the worse.

THE opera's never over until the fat lady sings.

IF the epileptic fits, wear it.

TWO can live as cheaply as one, but for half as long.

THERE are three kinds of women, the beautiful, the intelligent and the majority.

THERE are three kinds of men, the handsome, the caring and the majority.

THERE are three kinds of mathematicians, those who can count, and those who can't.

THE advance of science is measured at the rate which exceptions to the rules accumulate.

NOTHING carries gossip faster than a sour grapevine.

IT is easy, the night before, to get up early next morning.

GETTING up in the morning is simply a matter of mind over mattress.

NOTHING beats a cold shower before breakfast, except no cold shower before breakfast.

SOME people have eyes but do not see, others have ears but do not hear, but none have tongues that talk not.

YOU may be able to read someone like a book, but you can't shut them up so easily.

A CLOSED mouth gathers no feet.

THE person who loses his head is usually the last to miss it.

DO not adjust your mind. The fault is with reality.

MONTY is a poor loser. But when have you ever met a rich one?

EVERYTHING was so different before it was all changed.

TIME wounds all heels.

TIME is nature's way of stopping everything from happening at once.

A CULT is a group too small to be a minority.

ALL babies are subject to change without notice.

SILENCE isn't always golden...sometimes it's guilt.

STREAKERS beware! Your end is in sight.

STREAK, or forever hold your piece.

DIPLOMACY is the art of saying "nice doggie" until you can find a rock.

MANY electricians make light work.

TODAY is tomorrow's yesterday.

GIVE masochists a fair crack of the whip.

I USED to be indecisive. But now I'm not so sure.

NEWTON was wrong. The earth sucks.

FIGHT poverty. Throw stones at beggars.

THOSE sadists sure know how to hurt a bloke.

ONE good thing about dog turds is that they keep people off the streets.

TOILET seats are worth every penny spent on them.

IF you sprinkle when you twinkle,
   be a sweetie and wipe the seatie.

As the wise man said

AS a wise man once said: Dead pigeons never fly at night. Drop these one-liners before your listeners have had too much to drink. Even sober they will probably need time to ponder their profundity. There is nothing rude in this section, intentionally so, to enable you to deliver them with an air of philosophical authority.

Just look them straight in the eye and say: "As a wise man told me ..."

WISDOM consists of knowing when to avoid perfection.

WE all admire the wisdom of those who ask us for advice.

UNILATERAL withdrawal is the answer to the population explosion.

YOU don't get a second chance to make a first impression.

IF you cannot say what you mean, you will never mean what you say.

YOU should always be sincere, whether you mean it or not.

THERE is nothing like horse riding to make a person feel better off.

PUNCTUALITY is something that, if you've got it, there are few to share it with.

TIME is nature's way of stopping everything from happening at once.

OFTEN he who hesitates, is glad he did.

A WISE man never laughs at his wife's old clothes.

IF you consult enough experts you can confirm any opinion.

TO decide not to decide is a decision. To fail to decide is a failure.

ASKING dumb questions is easier than correcting dumb mistakes.

THE key to success is to create a need and fill it.

THE fat person walks in the middle of the hall.

HARA-KIRI takes a lot of guts.

EDUCATION is what you get when you read the fine print. Experience is what you get from not reading it.

THE human body is a strange phenonemon. A pat on the back can often result in a swollen head.

A PAT on the back is only a few centimetres from a kick in the bum.

WHEN people are free to do as they please, they usually imitate each other.

MOST well-trodden paths lead nowhere.

NUCLEAR waste fades your genes.

SHAKESPEARE married the Avon lady.

FLIES spread disease, so keep yours shut.

AN antique vase may not be as old as it's cracked up to be.

NOTHING prompts payment of an old dentist bill like a new toothache.

AN auction is the only place you get something for nodding.

BETTER to remain silent and be thought a fool, than to speak out and remove all doubt.

THE best prophet of the future is the past.

BY failing to prepare, you are preparing to fail.

IF you can smile when things go wrong, then you must have someone in mind to blame.

THE best thing about bright ideas is that anyone can have them.

THINGS are getting so bad so quickly that the Good Old Days seem only a week old.

REALITY is a nice place to visit, but you surely wouldn't want to live there.

SOMEONE who thinks logically is a nice contrast to the real world.

IF you think there is good in everybody, then you haven't met everybody.

FRIENDS may come and go, but enemies accumulate.

REMEMBER, it is easier to find a travelling companion than to get rid of one.

EVERYONE is a genius at least once a year. A real genius has his ideas closer together.

IN every work of genius we recognise our rejected thoughts.

I REACH a conclusion whenever I am tired of thinking.

HE who lives upon hope will die fasting.

YOU can't tell which way the train went by looking at the track.

ALL generalisations are false. Including this one.

CHANGE is inevitable. Except from a vending machine.

DON'T take lateral thinking lying down.

IF you manage to keep calm when all around you are hysterical, then you don't understand the situation.

IF you are confused, you are simply misinformed.

THE best Post-Impressionists were tall, thin Poles.

I HAVE seen the truth, and it makes no sense.

OLD professors never die. They just lose their faculties.

AS the wise man said: "I hardly ever equivocate."

YESTERDAY is experience, tomorrow is hope. Today is getting from one to the other as best we can.

TOMORROW will be an action replay.

YOU have arrived if the meeting cannot start until you have arrived.

ANOTHER place that seems to arrive almost before you get started is the bridge that you were going to cross when you got to it.

IT'S rough travelling behind someone who never leaves a stone unturned.

ONLY a pessimist complains about the noise when opportunity knocks.

OPPORTUNITY is a good deal more conspicuous on the way out than on the way in.

TRUTH is stranger than fiction because one needs to stick to what you can make people believe.

It's not so much the work I like,
it's the people I run into

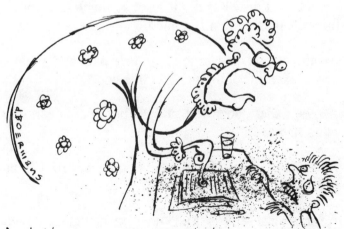

I've told you 30,000 times, stop exaggerating

Quotes from the famous and infamous

QUOTES from the famous, the not-so-famous and even the downright obscure are always valuable because you can shift the blame and attribute them to somebody else.

MONTY says speeches should be like women's skirts. Long enough to cover the subject and short enough to stimulate interest.

CONFUCIUS, he say too much.

AS Daniel said when he entered the lion's den: "Whoever does the after-dinner speaking, it won't be me."

AS Bruce Lee said when hit with a brick: "What Kung Fu Dat?"

AS the taxi driver said: "It's not so much the work I like, it's the people I run into."

AS the osteopath said to his female patient: "What's a joint like this doing in a girl like you?"

AS the fisherman's wife said: "Not tonight dear, I've got a haddock."

AS Monty said: "If you can lend me $10 I'll be everlastingly indebted to you."

AS the priest said: "We all know you can't take it with you, so if you place it on the collection plate I will see that it is sent on ahead."

AS the Romans said: "You've got to hand it to Venus de Milo."

AS General Custer said: "Look at all those darn Indians."

AS the Mayor of Hiroshima said: "What the bloody hell was that noise?"

AS the tutor said: "I've told you 30,000 times, stop exaggerating."

AS the tourist said to the porter: "Call me a taxi."
  The porter replied, "You're a taxi."

AS Snow White said: "I thought 7-Up was a soft drink until I discovered gin."

AS the Floozie said: "If I'm not in bed by midnight I'm going home."

AS Miss Murphy said when she found she was pregnant: "Heck, I hope it's mine."

AS the blonde said when the police raided the orgy. "What's wrong? Haven't you blokes seen 23 people in love before?"

AS the deaf nymphomaniac said: "Come again?"

Amazing information

IT can help the speaker to create a breathing space with an announcement of profound truth, like some of these items of useless information.

GEORGE Orwell wrote a novel for dyslexics called 1948.

MEDICAL science has just discovered that the real reason conception involves millions of sperm and just a single egg is that sperm will never stop and ask for directions.

THE bathtub was invented in 1850 and the telephone in 1875. If you had lived in 1850 you could have sat in the bath for 25 years without having to get out and answer the phone.

IT is not commonly known that Alexander Graham Bell actually invented two telephones.

IF it wasn't for Edison we'd all be watching television by candlelight.

I HAVE it on irrefutable authority that the best thing that can be said about the advent of motoring is that it has stamped out horse-stealing.

NEVER put milk in your cup before the tea. It is extremely unlucky. My grandfather always put the milk in first and over the course of eighty years all his teeth fell out.

TO discover which pickled onions are legitimate, unscrew the lid, turn the jar upside down and all the little bastards will drop out.

THE Magna Carta ensures that no free man can ever be hanged twice for the same offence.

DO you know that if 97,505,703 people died, I'd be next in line to the throne.

DID you know that Sir Francis Drake circumcised the world with a hundred foot clipper?

ACCORDING to the latest magazine in the doctor's waiting room President Kennedy has been shot while on a motor cavalcade through Dallas.

BEFORE the development of modern transport and communications, half the world didn't know how the other half lived. Today, in our enlightened age, half the world doesn't care.

IF you rest your hands on your chin when you are thinking, it keeps your mouth shut and you can't interrupt yourself.

ONE way to get a thick pile on your carpet is to invite an elephant into your lounge.

BUT show me a home where the buffallo roam and I'll show you a house full of shit.

Murphy's Law

MURPHY'S Law, which states that if anything can go wrong, it will, can be philosophically summarised in two words: Shit Happens.There are considerable extended versions:

TWO wrongs are only the beginning.

IF you are right no-one remembers. If you are wrong no one forgets.

A CLEAN tie attracts the soup of the day.

WHEN you know the right answers, nobody asks you the right questions.

ONLY your fussiest aunt will get the chipped cup or the glass with lipstick on it.

IF it says: "One size fits all," it won't fit anyone.

EVERY time you make ends meet, someone moves the ends.

THERE is always one more imbecile than you counted on.

MAKE it idiot-proof and somebody will make a better idiot.

THE summer hotel may be crowded, but there is always room for one bore.

OF two possible outcomes, only the worst will occur.

THERE is no job so simple that it cannot be ballsed up.

ALL inanimate objects can move just enough to get in your way.

IF your project doesn't work, look for the part you thought wasn't important.

THE one who says it cannot be done should never interrupt the one who is doing it.

THE day you'd sell your soul for something, souls are a glut.

WHICHEVER way you turn, when entering an elevator, the buttons are on the other side.

THE hardness of the butter is in direct proportion to the softness of the bread roll.

THERE is nothing so small it cannot be blown out of proportion.

THERE is no limit to how bad things can get.

ALMOST anything is easier to get into than to get out of.

THOSE who live closest arrive last.

NO one is listening, until you make a mistake.

SUCCESS always occurs in private, while failure happens in full public view.

AN error in the premise will appear in the conclusion.

ANY simple problem can be made insoluble if enough meetings are held to discuss it.

IF an hour has been spent amending a sentence, someone will move to delete the paragraph.

THE length of a progress report is inversely proportional to the amount of progress.

WHERE there's a will, there's a won't.

THE ideal applicant will turn up one day after the
position has been filled.

URGENCY varies inversely to importance.

THE bag that breaks is the one with the eggs.

THE severity of the itch is inversely proportional to
reach.

THE colder the X-ray table the more of your body is
required on it.

INTERCHANGEABLE parts won't.

NO two identical parts are alike.

TEMPORARY projects become permanent and permanent jobs become all too temporary.

THE more trivial the research the more people will
read it and agree, the more crucial the research the less
it will be read and understood.

IF you file it you will know where it is and never need
it. If you don't file it you will need it and never know
where it is.

A FREE agent is anything but.

THERE'S never time to do it right, but always time to do it again.

IN every hierarchy each employee tends to rise to the level of his incompetence.

THE person working on the problem is the one who is absent.

THE solving of a problem lies in finding the solvers.

THE chief cause of problems is solutions.

WHEN a problem goes away the people working to solve it do not.

AFTER the project is completely stuffed, all those who initially endorsed it will say they wished they had voiced their reservations at the time.

CHIPPED dishes never break.

EVERYONE has a scheme that will not work.

THE one who does the least work will get the most credit.

AS soon as you make a cup of hot coffee the boss will ask you to do something which will last until the coffee is cold.

IF something is confidential it will be left in the photocopier.

IF anything is used to its full potential, it will break.

THAT which cannot be taken apart will fall apart.

EXCEPTIONS always outnumber the rules.

YOU discover something has gone wrong only when you make an odd number of mistakes.

IF you understand it, it's obsolete.

WIND velocity increases in direct relation to the cost of the hairdo.

WHEN you have been waiting in a long queue the people immediately behind you will be shunted to a new queue.

EXPERIENCE is something you don't get until just after you need it.

ANY bureaucracy reorganised to streamline efficiency is immediately indistinguishable from its predecessor.

PAY checks and love letters arrive three weeks late while junk mail arrives the day it was posted.

WHEN you drop change at a vending machine the cents will fall at your feet and the dollars will roll out of sight.

THE benefits of Murphy's Law: Nobody notices the big errors.

MURPHY'S Law was not propounded by Murphy, but by another bloke of the same name.

AND one from Flannigan: Murphy was an optimist!

Words

IF lawyers are disbarred and clergymen defrocked, does it follow that electricians are delighted, musicians denoted, cowboys deranged, models deposed, composers decomposed, tree surgeons debarked and dry cleaners depressed?

IS there a word in the English language that contains all the vowels? Unquestionably.

TWO monologues do not make a dialogue.

THE longest word in the English language is the one following the phrase: "And now a word from our sponsor."

FRED always called a spade a spade, until the night he fell over a fuckin' shovel.

A CHRYSANTHEMUM by any other name would be easier to spell.

PROCRASTINATION is the thief of time, especially if you can't spell it.

NOW let's get some words in alphabetical order:

ARROGANCE is too often the companion of celebrity.

ATHEISM is simply divine.

BARBARISM drives me wild.

CARAVANS are a drag.

CANNIBALS are not vegetarians. They are humanitarians.

CATARRH really gets up my nose.

CIRCUMCISIONS alter cases.

CONFUSION creates jobs.

CORRUGATED iron is really groovy.

DEFEATISM will always get the better of me.

ENEMAS really put the wind up me.

EPILEPSY has me in fits.

EQUESTRIANS ask too many questions.

ESCHATOLOGY will be the death of me.

HERMAPHRODITES can't have it both ways.

HYPODERMICS really get under my skin.

I COULDN'T care less about indifference.

I DON'T enjoy being a hedonist.

I'D give anything to be a philanthropist.

I'D give my right arm to be a concert pianist.

I'VE got my doubts about scepticism.

KEEP your introspection to yourself.

MASOCHISTS need a good hiding.

MUTATE now and avoid the rush.

PROCRASTINATE now!

SADISM really cuts me up.

SATYRS should stop acting the goat.

SMOKING shortens your cigarettes.

SKINHEADS have more hair than brains.

SPEECH therapists are all talk.

THERE is no future in Existentalism.

WHITHER Atrophy. See *Dabbler's Dictionary*, page 273

Life

SUCCESS in life depends on two things, luck and pluck. And luck depends on finding someone to pluck. Here are some more golden rules of life:

WHOEVER has the gold makes the rules.

LIFE is what you do before you die.

LIFE. The first half is ruined by our parents, the second half by our children.

LIFE begins at forty, but so does lumbago, bad eyesight, arthritis and the habit of telling the same story three times.

LIFE is a near death experience.

THE first three minutes of your life can be the most dangerous. The last three minutes can be pretty dodgy as well.

ONE of the hardest decisions of life is when to start middle age.

MIDDLE age is when you are sitting at home on Saturday night and the phone rings and you hope it isn't for you.

LIFE is what happens to us while we are making other plans.

JUST when we thought we knew all the answers, life starts asking the wrong questions.

YOU get halfway through it before you realise life is not a dress rehearsal.

IF you think life is a joke consider the punchline.

THE only people who will find what they are looking for in life will be the fault-finders.

LIFE is like an ashtray, full of little doubts.

LIFE can only be understood backwards, but it must be lived forewards.

LIVE life so that no matter what happens, it couldn't happen to a nicer person.

LIVE each day as if it is your last, and one day it will.

ALL my life I have been doubtful. Now I'm not so sure.

BETTER to be a coward for a minute than dead for the rest of your life.

THERE is not one shred of evidence to support the notion that life is serious.

LIFE can be summed up in three words: It goes on.

LIFE is a play. And it's not it's length but it's perform-ance that counts.

ONE of life's difficult decisions is trying to pick the shortest queue at the check-out counter.

LIFE can be a bed of roses, and full of pricks.

VIRGINITY is just a bubble on the stream of life, one prick and it's gone forever.

LIFE is a sexually transmitted disease.

LIFE, we will never get out of it alive.

ONE of the rules of life is, those playing leap frog must complete all jumps.

DEATH is nature's way of telling you to slow down.

Mixed metaphors

A colourful Australian politician, Sir Joh Bjelke-Petersen, became notorious for his mixed metaphors.During his long political career he spawned dozens of comical imitators who reinforced his image as the politician who would always "keep his nose to the grindstone", and who warned reporters that "from now on I am watching everything you do with a fine toothcomb." Here are some of his and many others:

WE'LL burn that bridge when we come to it.

HE'S up the tree without a paddle.

HE'S the type who will cut your throat behind your back.

DON'T throw the garbage out with the bathwater.

MY opponents are using a sledge hammer to grind their political axes.

IT'S time to grab the bull by its tail and look it squarely in the eye.

HE is burning the midnight oil from both ends.

EVERYTHING goes hand and foot together.

WE took the thunder out of his sails.

JUST wait until the shoe fits the other foot.

IF we don't watch out they will pull the rug from under us in midstream.

WHEN he finds out what you've done the sparks will hit the fan.

IT will only take ten minutes if you could walk as the crow flies.

HE'S flying against the current.

PEOPLE are dying like hotcakes.

DON'T kiss a gift horse in the mouth.

HE insisted he was not talking through rose coloured glasses.

HE took to it like a duck out of water.

THE busy administration staff said they would be burning the midnight oil from 8pm to 10.30pm.

SOME are in the fast lane while most of us are peddling along on our skate boards.

KINDLY adjust your dress before leaving as a refusal often offends.

people are dying like hotcakes

2
Professionals and the Business World

IN the business world the executive knows something about everything, the technician knows everything about something, and the phone receptionist knows everything. That's office politics.

Business

A MAN is known by the company he floats.

WHY don't efficiency experts go into business themselves and make a fortune?

THE only person who got all of his work done by Friday was Robinson Crusoe.

FRANKLY, if you laid out all the managing directors end to end, they still wouldn't reach a decision.

EVERY organisation has an allotted number of positions to be filled by misfits, and once a misfit leaves, another will be recruited.

AN economist is an expert who will know tomorrow

49

why the trends he predicted yesterday didn't happen today.

PROSPERITY is something businessmen create and politicians take the credit for.

IF the economy is really bouncing back, why are so many cheques doing the same?

THE time spent on making progress reports restricts the time allocated for progress, so stability is achieved when all time is spent reporting on the lack of progress.

EVEN Tarzan used to come home exhausted, flop into the arm chair and say: "Jane, it's a jungle out there!"

SUCCESS is like smoking dope. The more you suck the higher you get.

A CLIENT phoned to ask what time the store opened. "What time can you get here?" replied the owner.

A BUSINESSMAN can't win these days. If he does something wrong he's fined, if he does something right, he's taxed.

BUSINESS is so bad these days even those people who don't pay are not buying.

LAST year it was my doctor who put me on a diet. This year it was my accountant.

AN income is what you can't live without, or within.

IN our business we are now at the bridge we were going to cross when we came to it.

AS the hooker said to her client: "It's a business to do pleasure with you."

THE prayer of the destitute prostitute: "And now I lay me down too cheap."

WOMEN can go out and give it away
But they'll be arrested if they do it for pay.

THE overworked prostitute made two appointments for the same time. She managed to squeeze them both in.

Bosses

THE boss is the bloke in the office who is late when you are early, and early when you are late.

YES-MEN are staffers who hang around the man nobody "no's."

IF at first you don't succeed, you're probably not related to the boss.

IS there anything more embarrassing than watching the boss do something you told him couldn't be done?

THE boss said it was just a suggestion, and that nobody had to follow it, unless they wanted to keep their jobs.

"HAVE you an opening for a genius?"

"Yes," said the boss, "and don't slam it on the way out."

WHEN my boss says he would welcome an exchange of opinion he means I should arrive with mine and go away with his.

A BOSS is someone who delegates authority, shifts blame and takes credit.

"YES, you can have the job as my assistant, but I don't want a yes-man, so get that straight from the start."

AN executive is one who can take three hours for lunch without hindering production.

WHEN I say he's a born executive I mean his father owns the business.

WHEN it comes to qualifications it's hard to beat having a father who owns the company.

CHAIRMAN: "Let's take a vote. All against raise their hands and say 'I resign'."

WHEN the sweet young wife met the chief executive she gushed: "Oh, so you're John's boss. He's always talking about you Mr Slavedriver."

"JUST because I made love to you last night, who said you could come in late?" said the boss sternly.

"My solicitor," said his secretary.

Office

COMPUTERS will never replace human stupidity.

A SECRETARY is someone you pay to learn to type while she looks for a husband.

SHE said she could handle 30 words a minute.
  "Shorthand?"
  "No. Reading," she said.

EVER since the boss told his secretary that he was a stickler for punctuation she hasn't been late once.

Money

THRIFT is the most admirable virtue in any ancestor.

MISERS aren't much fun to live with, but they do make wonderful ancestors.

THE difference between a wanker and a banker is that the wanker knows what he is doing.

MONEY used to talk. Now it goes without saying.

MONEY doesn't always bring happiness. People with ten million are no happier than people with nine million.

MONEY can't buy happiness, but it helps you look for it in a lot more places.

MONEY doesn't go as far as it used to, yet it goes faster.

53

A MONEY grabber is anyone who can grab more money than you.

MONEY isn't everything. It isn't even enough!

MONEY won't help you make friends, but you will have a better class of enemies.

THE bank is an institution where you can borrow money, provided you can show sufficient evidence that you don't need it.

BUDGET is a form of worrying before you spend instead of after.

IT is my wife who makes the budget work. We simply go without a lot of things I don't need.

A CREDITOR has a better memory than a debtor.

THE Irish call their basic currency the punt because it rhymes with bank manager.

MORE often than not bankruptcy is due to a lack and a lass.

IT'S no disgrace to be born poor. It's no disgrace to die poor. But in between it doesn't hurt to be rich.

MAN to bank manager, "How do I stand for a loan?"
    "You don't, you kneel."

A FOOL and his money soon go partying.

A FOOL and his money are soon popular.

HAVE you ever wondered why a fool and his money are never there when you need a loan?

A FOOL and his money were lucky to get together in the first place.

A WIDOW and her money are soon married.

NOW is the time to be frugal at any cost.

I MARRIED my wife for her money. And believe me I've earned it.

I MADE my money in the old fashioned way. I inherited it.

MY uncle makes money the old fashioned way. He steals it.

YOUR income is the amount of money you spend more than.

IF only philanthropists would give it back to the same people they took it from.

IF you lend a friend five dollars and never see him again, it was worth it.

"HAVE you forgotten that five dollars I lent you?"
  "No, not yet, give me time."

A BARGAIN is something you can't use but which is so cheap you can't afford not to buy it.

YOUNG Johnny decided against putting money in his piggy bank. He said it turned kids into misers and parents into bank robbers.

HE'S such a brilliant accountant they have just named a loophole after him.

THE man who writes the bank's advertisments is certainly not the same bloke who lends the money.

WHEN it comes to giving to charity, some people stop at nothing.

WHEN the lass was told her $100 note was a forgery she cried: "Oh no. I've been raped again."

A FINANCIALLY astute hooker who works around the stock exchange is known as Cash Flo.

SHE told her banker she didn't have much collateral, but would he care to take one of her promiscuity notes.

THE cop asked if he could describe the missing treasurer.
   "Yes, he's six foot tall and $100,000 short."

A DIVIDEND is per centum, per annum, perhaps.

A PREFERENTIAL creditor is the first bloke to be told there's no money left.

ECONOMIC forecasters are forthright. They manage to get one in four right.

ALWAYS borrow money from a pessimist. He doesn't expect to get it back.

THERE are many things money can't buy, including what it used to.

ACCORDING to the collector, some people pay when due, some overdue, some never do. How do you do?

WHEN it comes to giving money, some people stop at nothing.

IT is much better to give than receive, and it's deductible.

THE trouble with some people who give until it hurts is that they are so sensitive to pain.

THE cost of living is killing me.

THE meaning of the three balls over the pawnshop is that it's two-to-one you won't get your money back.

REMEMBER, the darkest hour is just before the pawn.

A SAILOR who was asked how he spent his pay said some went on booze, some on women and he squandered the rest.

MY uncle is so rich that when he writes a cheque the bank bounces.

AN economist is the bloke who can save money by cutting down some other person's expense.

AN economist is one who marries Elle Macpherson for her money.

A CHARTERED accountant is an undertaker who has had a charisma bypass.

HE had always tried to pay his bills with a smile. But invariably they wanted money.

THE accountant reported that last year the company was poised on the edge of a precipice. "But this year we made a great leap forward."

WITH the New World Order the USA will from now on be known as the IOUSA.

THE wealthy financier took a tumble for a blonde and lost his balance at the bank.

HE said: "I would go through anything with you?"
    "Good," she replied, " let's start with your bank account."

"DEAR Mr Fink," read the bank statement, "After checking our records we find we have done more for you than your own mother did. We have carried you for 15 months."

EVEN the oldest profession runs on a tight fiscal policy. When her regular client asked for credit she said: "No way, John. You are into me far too much already."

58

Taxes

THE difference between cheating on your wife and cheating on the taxman is that when you get caught the taxman still wants to screw you.

THERE is one consolation about life and taxes. When you are through with one, you are through with the other.

IT'S a good thing we don't pay taxes on what we think we are worth.

WHOEVER said you couldn't be wounded by a blank obviously hasn't received a taxation form.

Success

SUCCESS is relative. The more success the more relatives.

YOU have reached the pinnacle of success when you are uninterested in money, compliments or publicity.

YOU have arrived when the meeting can't start until you have arrived.

YOU are making progress if every mistake you make is a new one.

YOU'LL never lead the band if you can't face the music.

FORGET the past. Nobody becomes successful in the past.

BE awfully nice to them on the way up, you may need them on the way down.

NOBODY has more ups and downs than the person in the end seat at the theatre.

A GO-GETTER is the man who can get his elbows on both armrests of the theatre seat.

Jobs

IN most early conversations the subject will turn to: "What do you do for a crust?" Let it be a trigger to drop a one-liner.

I WORK at the circus where I circumcise the elephants. The pay's not much but the tips are enormous.

I'VE decided to leave, I'm going around in circles and it's a dead-end job.

I'VE always wanted to be a comedian, but I'm frightened people will laugh at me.

I WAS destined to be a travel writer. My first job was a proofreader for a skywriting firm.

HE'S a doorman because he wanted a job with plenty of openings.

ON his first day as a doorman he got arrested for loitering.

HE got fired after a week as a street sweeper because he couldn't keep his mind on the gutter.

IT takes him an hour to get to work, and that's well after he gets to the factory.

MONTY had a job painting white lines down the middle of the road, but it sent him around the bend.

HE left his job in a factory which made parking meters. There was nowhere to park.

SHE got a job as a public relations officer in the tampon factory. She puts a get well card in every packet.

MY father used to be a blacksmith in a butcher shop. He used to shoo flies.

MY uncle is an espionage agent at the mint. He's a mint spy.

MY brother is a police reporter. Once a week he has to report to the police.

HIS new job is touting for a doctor. He goes around making people sick.

ALRIGHT, you are an actor. But what do you do for a living?

THE police poster said: Man wanted for robbery in Dublin. Paddy said if it was in Donegal he would take it.

CECIL has a good job at the gay bar. He examines the prospective members.

HE has a job driving away customers. He's a taxi driver.

HE wanted to be a sex maniac, but the competition was too stiff.

CYNTHIA works as a receptionist at a hotel and gets half board. Fifi works in a massage parlour and gets her whole board.

A BLOW job is better than no job.

On work itself

MOST young blokes stop looking for work the moment they get a job.

ALL work and no play makes Jack a dull boy; and Jill a wealthy widow.

HARD work never killed anybody, but it frightens some people half to death.

VARIETY may be the spice of life, but it's good old monotony that buys the groceries.

WORK, I love it. I could stand and watch it all day.

WHEN the boss asked the prospective labourer how much money he expected to earn, Murphy replied: "All of it."

YOU know the interview is not going well when the boss makes a paper aeroplane out of your application form.

IF a job's worth doing it's worth making sure that everyone knows that you're doing it.

Consultants

A CONSULTANT is someone who takes the watch off your wrist and then tells you what time it is.

A CONSULTANT is simply a professional who can't find a job of his own.

A CONSULTANT knows a hundred ways of making love, but is still a virgin.

ANY fool can consult, and many of them do.

THOSE that can are doers, those that can't are consultants.

3
Matters of Justice

Courts and the law

JUSTICE and law are distant cousins and usually they are not on speaking terms.

LAW clerk Lil, on a summer's night,
   Turned down the motel's bedroom light,
   The judge beside her, whispered things,
   Of wedding bells and diamond rings,
   He spoke his love in burning phrase,
   Made love in forty foolish ways,
   Til he left to place the breakfast order
   And Lil turned off the tape recorder.

THE court is a place where justice is dispensed with.

AN appeal is when you ask one court to show its contempt for another.

JUDGE: "There is far too much sexual deviance going on. And I'm not having it."

THE judge he populates the city jails by grave decisions, heads or tails.

A JUDGE is a man who ends a sentence with a sentence.

RON the Con approached the bench and said: "Judge, give me a sentence with the word freedom in it."

HE threw himself on the mercy of the court, and missed.

LAG: "Sorry, I was as drunk as a judge."
   Judge: "Surely you mean as drunk as a lord?"
   "Yes, my lord."

THE lawyer asked the damsel to repeat the words the defendant had used. She refused, saying that they were not fit to be heard by a gentleman.
   "Then whisper them to the judge," he said.

IT'S illegal to make liquor privately, and to make water publicly.

IF the facts are against you, argue the law. If the law is against you, argue the facts.

A BAD compromise beats a good courtcase.

A JURY is twelve people who will try anyone once.

LAG: "As God is my judge I am not guilty."
   Judge: "He's not. I am. You are. Three years!"

JUDGE: "Are you trying to show contempt for this court?"
   Defence lawyer: "No. I'm trying to hide it."

A JURY is twelve people chosen to decide who has the better lawyer.

THE judge demanded to know why the accused had absconded. "It was the only sound advice I could give him," said his lawyer.

"COULDN'T you have settled this out of court?"
  "That's what we were doing when the police interfered."

THE jury is one thing that never works properly once it's been fixed.

A BRIBE is when the giver says "thanks," and the receiver says "don't mention it."

IT takes a thief to catch a thief, and a jury to let him go.

"HAVE you ever been cross-examined before?"
  "Yes, Yer Honour, I'm a married man."

"DO you plead guilty or not guilty?"
  "What else have you got?"

"DO you plead guilty or not guilty?"
  "How do I know. I haven't heard the evidence yet."

"HAVE you anything to offer before judgement is passed?"
  "No Yer Honour. My lawyer has left me skint."

"GUILTY! Ten days or $200 dollars."
  "I'll take the two hundred, thanks Judge!"

"ORDER! Order in the court."
"Whisky on the rocks for me, thanks."

"YOU are charged with habitual drunkeness, what is your excuse?"
"Habitual thirst, Yer Worship."

"IS this the first time you have been up before me?" said the judge to the old lag.
"I dunno," he replied. "What time do you get up?"

"OPEN up. It's the CIB."
"Can you spell that please?"

"THIS pen leaks," said the prisoner, as the rain came through the roof.

DAD is popular in prison. He is the lifer of the party.

Lawyers

THE difference between a hooker and a lawyer isn't much, except the hooker will stop screwing you when you're dead.

WE know a funeral director who buries lawyers in holes fifty metres deep. Because deep down they are good people.

HOW many lawyer jokes are there? Only three. The others are true stories.

I WANTED to be a lawyer but they found out my mother and father were married.

IF there had never been any lawyers, there would never have been any need for them.

TALK is cheap, until you talk to a lawyer.

LAWYER: "I charge $300 to answer three questions."
  "That's steep isn't it?"
  "It is. And what is your final question?"

A LAWYER is a man who helps you get what's coming to him.

OLD lawyers never die. They just lose their appeal.

IF you can't get a lawyer who knows the law, get one who knows the judge.

THE definition of utter waste is a bus full of lawyers going over a cliff with three empty seats.

IS a lady barrister without briefs a solicitor?

BLONDES make better barristers because they never lose their appeal.

WHAT do you call a lawyer with an IQ of 25?
  Your Honour.

THE difference between a lawyer and a football is that you only get six points for kicking a football between the uprights.

THE difference between a catfish and lawyer is that one is a scum-sucking bottom dweller and the other is a fish.

ASKED why the university was experimenting on lawyers instead of rats the scientist replied: "Well, you know how it is. You get so attached to rats."

4
Health, Both Mind and Body

Health

THE human body, with proper care, will last a life-time.

A MINOR operation is one which is carried out on someone else.

MOST health concerns about coffee are groundless.

HAPPY people resist disease better than unhappy people. In other words, the surly bird catches the germ.

THE art of medicine consists of humouring the patient while nature cures the disease.

THERE are several stages of sickness; ill, pill, bill and sometimes will.

SECONDS count, especially when dieting.

HE hasn't fully recovered from his operation. He still has two more payments to go.

LIFE is a hereditary disease. And terminal.

THEY are so healthy where I come from that we had to shoot a bloke to start a cemetery.

WHEN the bottom has fallen out of your world, take milk of magnesia and watch the world fall out of your bottom.

THERE are probably better cures for a cold than three whiskies, but who cares.

THE doctor put Teresa on the pill. But she said it was no good. It kept falling out.

IF the human brain was simple enough for us to understand, we'd be so simple we couldn't.

A FERTILE imagination is no compensation for vasectomy.

THERE is a clear difference between cholesterol and fat.
    You can hardly wake up in the morning with half a cholesterol.

THE Irish are great believers in health. They are always drinking to other people's.

A GOOD many people commit suicide with a knife and fork.

PEOPLE who say they are going on a diet are just wishful shrinkers. Or they're thick, and tired of it.

DIETICIANS are living off the fat of the land.

SKIPPING is the best way to lose weight; skip lunch, then skip dinner and skip desserts.

THE best reducing exercise is to put both hands on the dinner table and push backwards.

THE most difficult part of a diet is not watching what you eat, it's watching what other people eat.

SHE said that on his latest diet her husband lost five pounds a week. In 18 months she hopes to be rid of him altogether.

THE hypochondriac lift driver was a worrier. He kept thinking he was coming down with something.

SHE visited the doctor for the fifth time that week: "It's awful," she said. "The pain comes every 20 minutes and lasts for an hour."

A HYPOCHONDRIAC broods over ill-health but never hatches a remedy.

THE hypochondriac had only four words on his tomb stone: "See, I told you."

I WOULD rather have a bottle in front of me than a frontal labotomy.

CANCER cures smoking.

SMOKING shortens your cigarettes.

HE has read so much about the effects of smoking that he has finally given up reading.

IT took a lot of will power, but finally he has given up trying to give up smoking.

"WILL you give up smoking for me?" she said.
  "Who says I've been smoking for you?" he said.

THEY were a perfect pair. He was a hypochondriac and she was a pill.

FRED thought he had a club foot for forty-two years. When he died they discovered he had his boots on the wrong feet.

A SIGN on the toilet door at the Sex Change Clinic says: "We may never piss this way again."

Fitness

I KEEP fit by wrestling, with my conscience.

MY wife keeps fit by jumping, to conclusions.

SHE was asked if her husband did any exercise.
  "Well, he was out last week five nights running."

WHEN you feel like you need more exercise, lie down until the feeling wears off.

MONTY took up exercise and now he has the energy of a man twice his age.

HIS doctor told him to play 36 holes a day, so he went out and bought a harmonica.

Hospitals

A HOSPITAL is a place where people who are run down generally wind up.

A HOSPITAL is a place where they wake you at five o'clock in the morning to give you a sleeping pill.

FRED was in hospital for a complicated operation.
    In fact, while he was in there the surgeon took his wife out.

SURGEON to his assistant as he begins an operation: "How's that for openers?"

DID you hear about the clumsy surgeon who was performing a vasectomy? He missed and got the sack.

IT is now suspected that doctors wear masks so that when anything goes wrong they can't be identified.

WHEN the X-ray specialist announced he was to marry one of his patients everyone wondered what he saw in her.

Doctors

NEVER wish a doctor a prosperous New Year.

A DOCTOR is a bloke who gets your wife to take her clothes off, then sends you the bill.

"OH, Doctor," she said coyly, "Where will I put my clothes?"

"Put them over there, next to mine!"

THERE is one advantage in being poor. Doctors will cure you faster.

THE doc said he would examine him for $50. The patient said if he could find it he'd go halves.

THE doctor felt the patient's thin purse and admitted there was nothing he could do.

WHAT'S the use of consulting a doctor when you have a cold when he gives you a heart attack with the bill?

THE patient said he thought he was suffering from amnesia, so the doctor asked for his bill in advance.

MY doctor doesn't believe in unnecessary surgery. Which means he doesn't operate unless he really needs the money.

SOME doctors are prepared to give the bad news face to face. Others prefer to send the bill by post.

"DOCTOR, can I have a second opinion?"
"Of course, come back tomorrow."

"DOCTOR, can I have a second opinion?"
"Of course. You're ugly too."

DOC: "Have you ever been incontinent?"
    Patient: "Nope. Never been interstate for that matter."

DOCTOR: "How's that man that swallowed the fifty cent piece?"
    Nurse: "Still no change."

THE young woman was worried. "Oh doctor, will the scar show?"
    "That, young lady," he said, "is up to you."

SHE told the doc she had a small embarrassing wart. The doc advised her to divorce him.

SHE asked if the pills were habit forming.
    "Rubbish," said the doc, "I've been taking them myself for years."

SHE asked the doctor: "What's the best thing to take when you are run down?"
    "The number of the bastard who hit you," he said.

"WELL, Doc, how do I stand?"
    "Damned if I know. It's a bloody miracle."

HE said he was having trouble with his breathing. The doc said he'd soon put a stop to that.

MURPHY was given two weeks to live. He decided to take one week in January and the other in March.

FLANNIGAN was given six months to live, but when he said he couldn't pay the bill the doctor gave him another six months.

76

HE complained to the doc that he had a terrible pain whenever he raised his arm.

"Well, don't raise your bloody arm," was the helpful advice.

EVEN on his holidays the workaholic gynaecologist used to look up his old girlfriends.

THE gynaecologist was also a home handyman. He not only wallpapered the hallway, but he did it through the front door letter box.

AFTER many years in the practice he described himself as a spreader of old wives' tails.

AND the deaf gynaeocologist was able to read lips.

DOCTORS have their admirers, indeed, some of their greatest followers are funeral directors.

Psychiatrists

SHRINKS are another phenomenon we all understand. Anybody who goes to a shrink needs their head read, but read on for more one-liners with which your listeners will identify.

PSYCHIATRY is the care of the id by the odd.

NEUROTICS build castles in the air. Psychotics live in them, and psychiatrists collect the rent.

YOU go to a psychiatrist when you feel slightly cracked and keep going until you're completely broke.

A PSYCHIATRIST is called a shrink because that's what he does to your wallet.

A PSYCHIATRIST is someone who will listen for hours, as long as you don't make sense.

A PSYCHIATRIST is a mental detective for mental defectives.

HE stopped going to his psychiatrist because he was being asked too many personal questions.

THE friendly psychiatrist is the one who lies on the couch with you.

THE patient said he had half a mind to become a schizophrenic.

HYPOCHRONDIA is the only disease I haven't got.

AS Dr Psych said: "I can guarantee a sure cure, or your mania back."

GOING to the psychiatrist didn't cure Monty's drinking problem. He kept falling off the couch.

THE patient feared he was losing his memory and he was worried about it.
   "Never mind, try to forget it," was the psych's advice.

HE said he was suffering from amnesia.
The doc said: "Have you ever had it before?"

MY shrink cured my problem. I was once too afraid to answer the phone. Now I answer it whether it rings or not.

"YOU don't have a complex at all, Mr Jones," said the psychiatrist, "actually, you are inferior."

"WHAT will I do for loss of memory?" asked the patient.
　"Pay me in advance," said the shrink.

A PSYCHIATRIST reported that half his patients went to him because they were not married. The other half went to him because they were.

THE dwarf told him he was worried because he weighed 50 kilos and his testicles weighed 25 kilos and he thought he was half nuts.

DID you hear about the psychiatrist who kept his wife under the bed because he thought she was a little potty?
　... or the psychiatrist who woke up under his bed and realised HE was a little potty.

"DOCTOR, Doctor," said the patient as he burst into the psychiatrist's room, "I feel invisible."
　"I'm sorry, but I can't see you know," said the shrink.

"DOC, I keep thinking that I am a pair of curtains."
　"Sit down and pull yourself together."

"DOC, my problem is, people keep ignoring me."
  "Next please."

HE walked into the clinic with a steering wheel in his hands. "I keep getting these funny turns," he said.

"HOW long has your wife thought she was a chicken?"
  "About 18 months."
  "Why didn't you come here earlier?"
  "We needed the eggs."

"NOW that I have cured you of your gambling addiction," said the psychiatrist, "I can present you with your bill."
  "Thanks Doc. Toss you double or nothing."

A FELLOW phoned his shrink. "Doctor, my wife needs help. She thinks she's a horse." When the doc said it could be a long and costly treatment the fellow replied: "Money is no object. She's won her last three starts!"

PATIENT: "Why do you think so many people take an instant dislike to me?"
  Psychiatrist: "Saves time."

PATIENT: "Everybody hates me."
  Psychiatrist: "Don't be silly. Everyone hasn't met you yet."

"DOC, my wife is a kleptomaniac."
  "Is she taking anything for it?"

"I THINK I am going mad, doctor. Every time I ask someone the time I get a different answer."

"I USED to suffer from a split personality, Doc, but now we're both okay!"

SHE took her husband to the psychiatrist. "He says he is suffering from hallucinations, but I'm sure he is only imagining it," she said.

HE asked to explain her dreams.
　　"I haven't had any this week, doctor," she said.
　　"Well how the hell can I help you if you don't do your homework?"

TWO psychos passed each other in the hospital corridor. One said: "You're feeling good, how am I?"

"I'VE got butterflies crawling all over me." said the patient.
　　"Well don't flick the bloody things all over me," said the psycho jumping away.

PSYCH: "So, you think you are a dog, eh? That's no problem. Just hop up on the couch."
　　Patient. "I can't. I'm not allowed."

"THERE is nothing physically wrong with your son, but I must tell you he has an Oedipus complex."
　　"Oedipush shiedipush, Just as long as he loves his Mummy."

HOW many psychiatrists does it take to change a light bulb. Only one. But the bulb must want to be changed.

THE psychiatrist had listened for ten minutes while his patient insisted he had turned into a bell.

"Take these pills. If they don't work, give me a ring!"

I TOLD my girlfriend I was seeing a psychiatrist. She told me she was seeing a psychiatrist, a footballer and two barmen.

"MR BROWN," said the woman psychiatrist, "you have acute paranoia".

"Thanks Doc, and your tits are not bad either!"

"IF these pills don't stop your kleptomania," said the psychiatrist, "try and get me a video recorder."

5
The Battle of the Sexes

Things sexual

WHERE would we be without sex? It wasn't the apple on the tree but the pair on the ground that caused all the trouble in the Garden of Eden and we haven't been able to get sex out of the system since.

AN erection is like the Theory of Relativity;
   the more you think about it the harder it gets.

SHORT skirts have a tendency to make men polite.
   Have you ever seen a bloke get on a bus ahead of one?

A LITTLE coitus never hoitus.

SEX is hereditary. If your parents never had it, chances are you won't either.

SOW your wild oats on Saturday night and pray for a crop failure on Sunday.

PORNOGRAPHY is in the groin of the beholder.

OBSCENITY is anything that gives the judge an erection.

SEX discriminates against the shy and the ugly.

LOVE your neighbour, but don't get caught.

LOVE is a matter of chemistry, sex is physics.

TWO'S company, three's the result.

SEX is a three-letter word desperate for a four-letter word.

SEX is one of the ten reasons for reincarnation. The other nine are unimportant.

DON'T do it if you can't keep it up.

IN court it takes twelve men to find out if a woman is innocent. In the back seat of a car it only takes one.

MAN cannot live on bread alone.He needs a bit of crumpet.

YOU can tell the sex of a chromosome by taking down its genes.

TO go together is blessed, to come together is divine.

MAKING love during the safe period is when her husband's away.

GET back to grass roots. Fornicate on the lawn.

SHE was virgin on the edge of intercourse.

ROSES are red, pansies are gay, if it wasn't for women we'd all be that way.

THEY did it 144 times, which was gross indecency.

ANNUAL sex orgy here on Friday. First served, first come.

ORAL sex is a taste of things to come.

ORAL sex! All she ever does is talk about it.

EIGHT-INCH pricks are just a phallusy.

POWER to the Peephole!

SEX Appeal. Give generously.

SADISM really cuts me up.

TRY the rhythm method. Root to music.

AVOID wet dreams. Sleep indoors.

HAVE a sex change. Swap your partner.

COPULATE on the carpet and have a matt finish.

LARGE cats are dangerous, but a little pussy never hurt anybody.

THE bi-sexual donkey had his hee in the morning and his haw at night.

A VAGINA that talks back to you is called an answering cervix.

MUSICIANS do it with an instrument.

CARPENTERS do it with their tools.

HANDYMEN do it with their hands.

LUMBERJACKS do it with their choppers.

CYCLISTS have it between their legs.

SQUASH players do it against the wall.

PSYCHIATRISTS do it on the couch.

TOWN planners do it with their eyes shut.

VICARS do it with their bishops.

I HAVE no aversions
    To mergin with virgins
    Tho' it's more fun to pet
    With a well-seasoned vet.

Women's perspective

IT is better to be looked over than overlooked.

LOVE is the triumph of imagination over intelligence.

LOVE is the delusion that one man differs from another.

VIRGINITY can be cured.

SEX has no calories.

SEX is like snow. You never know how many inches you are going to get or how long it will last.

A MAN in the house is worth two in the street.

WHAT matters is not the length of the wand, but the magic in the stick.

IT works better if you plug it in.

ORGASM is the gland finale.

THE best time to fake orgasm is when a Rottweiler is humping your leg.

MEN

IT seems natural to lump men, lazy bastards and condoms under the one heading because there is a natural link, and it saves space.

A SELF-MADE man is a horrible example of unskilled labour.

THE man who boasts that he is self-made should be given credit for not shifting the blame.

THE question is: Can a self-made man pull himself to pieces?

THE frustration the first time you can't make it the second time is nothing compared to the second time you can't make it the first time.

HE was wearing his Italian-style suit, with spaghetti bolognese all down the front.

HE'S discovered a new use for old clothes. He wears them.

HE has a suit for every day of the week, and he's wearing it.

HE had his dinner jacket on, with most of his dinner still on it.

MEN who put women on pedestals rarely knock them off.

"HOW long have you been wearing that corset, Harry?"
    "Ever since the wife found it in the car," he said.

HE was getting worried about the future. He was getting married in a month and he still hadn't found her a job.

MARRIED men have better halves, but bachelors have better quarters.

HE choses his own suits, but his wife picks his pockets.

THE upkeep of a wife is often the downfall of a husband.

A MAN never knows the value of a woman's love until he pays maintenance.

THE biggest stumbling block a man may have is the one under his hat.

FRED said he was a Women's Libber. "Yes, I want all women to be free. I hate it when they charge."

MEN have two reasons for staying at the pub all night. Either they've got no wives to go home to; or they have.

IF a bird craps on your car, never take her out again.

Lazy bastards

HE is so lazy he is dating a pregnant woman.

HE is so lazy he married a widow with three children.

HE even gets his wife to read the "Do It Yourself" book to him.

HE was so lazy he had his window box concreted over.

HE was so lazy he used to ride the underground in peak hours just to press his clothes.

THE only thing he ever took up at school was space.

THE only thing he has ever done to earn money was lose his baby teeth.

HE was born with a silver spoon in his mouth, and he hasn't stirred since.

HE is so lazy he won't even exercise discretion.

HE has invented a labour-saving device. It's called Tomorrow.

EVER since he was old enough to hold down a steady job, he hasn't.

HE doesn't know whether to work as a Coronation program seller or marriage guidance counsellor to the Pope.

SHE can tell by looking at her husband's face if he is lying.
    "Yes," she said, "If his lips are moving, he's lying."

DOES your husband lie awake at night?
    Yes, and he lies in his sleep, too.

Chauvinist pigs

TEN major reasons used by Chauvinst pigs to avoid marriage:
    I NEED time to think (meaning I need time to leave the country).

WOULDN'T it be wise to wait until you're pregnant?

I DON'T want to be tied down; unless it's with chains, cord and handcuffs.

WHAT would my wife say?

I'M a priest.

I CAN'T bear children.

I CAN'T bear you.

I'M wanted for murder in Queensland.

MY family has a history of madness.

BUT I'm not that stupid.

HE said he would like to see her in something long and flowing; like a river.

WHAT do you call a chauvinist pig doing the washing up? A start!

HE was glad when his wife became a feminist. Now she complains about all men, not just him.

HE thought sexual harassment was a pair of tight underpants.

THE odd thing about feminists is they want to get ahead in the office, but they resist advances.

YOU never hear of a man being asked how he combines marriage with a career.

I TOLD my wife I didn't believe in combining marriage and a career. Which is why I haven't worked since our wedding day.

INDEED, I believe women should be placed under a pedestal.

Condoms

THERE'S a new condom on the market for blokes over 60. It's called Software.

BUY condoms and avoid the issue.

BUY one condom for fun, buy 144 and be gross.

A CONDOM is like a sock in the puss.

IF the cap fits, wear it.

IN case of malfunction, marry.

MONTY put his condom on inside out and went.

MURPHY always puts on two. To be sure, to be sure.

AN entrepreneur is producing his own brand of condoms called Planned Parent Hood.

THE vending machine sign says: "If out of order, see publican. If it works, see barmaid."

HE wanted to know if Johnny Cash was the change from a vending machine.

WOMEN

GENERALLY speaking, women are generally speaking and would welcome an armoury of one-liners to keep the chauvinists in their place. Dare them to use the rude ones.

THE wisest of men can become foolish over women, while the most foolish of women is wise to men.

FOR every woman who makes a fool out of a man there is a woman who makes a man out of a fool.

THE clever woman is the one who knows how to give a man her own way.

NO woman is perfect. It's just compared to men they are.

WOMEN were born without a sense of humour so that they could love men and not laugh at them.

A SENSIBLE woman is more sensible than she looks because a sensible woman is too sensible to look sensible.

WHEN God created man, she was only joking.

MANY a woman has started out playing with fire and ended up cooking over it.

BEFORE you meet your handsome prince, you have to kiss a lot of toads.

THE waltz was invented by men, so that they could lead and step on a woman at the same time.

MEN say women can't be trusted too far. Women say men can't be trusted too near.

SHE was the kind of girl who didn't care for a man's company, unless he owned it.

DIETS are for women who are thick and tired of it.

WOMEN like the simple things in life, like men.

FRENCHMEN make the best lovers, but the Japanese make them smaller and cheaper.

NO man has ever stuck his hand up a skirt looking for a tram ticket.

"SEXY men are all alike," said Mabel.
   "Sexy men are all ah like too honey," said Lulubelle.

A VIRGIN is a nice girl that whispers sweet nothing-doings in your ear.

DO you know what virgins eat for breakfast?
   No. I didn't think you did.

IT is a woman's ambition to be weighed and found wanting.

GIRL talk: "Do you ever file your nails?"
   "No. I just cut them and throw them away."

"YOU know I never repeat gossip, so listen carefully, I will only say this once."

SHE said she hates repeating gossip. "But really, what else can you do with it?"

IF labour took as long as conception then birth could be over in a matter of seconds, and with no feeling whatsoever.

Women, from the male's perspective

IF you want to know why they're called the opposite sex, just express an opinion.

WOMEN should be obscene and not heard.

THE way to fight a woman is with your hat. Grab it and run.

THE first lie detector was made out of the rib of a man. And they have been unable to improve on that model ever since.

GIVE a woman an inch and she'll make a bathing costume.

A WOMAN wears a sweater to accentuate the positive and a girdle to eliminate the negative.

A SECRET is something a woman tells everybody not to tell anybody.

WOMEN do not believe everything they hear. But that doesn't prevent them from repeating it.

ROSE'S are red, Violet's are blue and Fifi isn't wearing any.

IF your wife wants to learn to drive, don't stand in her way.

IF you don't like the way women drive, then get off the footpath.

HIS wife has been booked so many times the cops have now given her a season's ticket.

WHEN a woman is looking for a husband she is either single or married.

MARIA Lotzabazooma has had eight husbands. Three of them were her own.

SOME women have been tried and found wanton.

THE richest floozie on Park Avenue wears mink all day and fox all night.

THE floozie failed her driving test. When the car stalled she got over into the back seat from force of habit.

Feminists

THERE'S too much history. How about herstory for a change?

LOVE is the delusion that one man is different from the rest.

THE way to a bloke's heart is through his stomach and, unfortunately, the way to his brain is through his underpants.

"FIRST I faked chastity," she said, "then I faked orgasm. And now I fake fidelity."

THE difference between a clitoris and a pub is simple. Most men know where to find a pub.

THE difference between a clitoris and a golf ball is that some blokes will spend up to 30 minutes looking for a golf ball.

IT'S a man's world. And the end is nigh.

EQUALITY is a myth. Women are superior.

A WOMAN who strives to be like a man lacks ambition.

THE only difference between men and pigs is that when pigs drink they don't make men of themselves.

MEN are like pigeons. They should never be looked up to.

STUPID men? That's tautology.

THE only things wives have in common with their husbands is that they were married on the same day.

SHE wanted a husband and put an advertisement in the Personal Column. She got 200 replies, all saying; "You can have mine."

GOD invented man because a vibrator can't mow the lawn.

SHE said she wouldn't mind having a baby, but unfortunately you have to marry one to get one.

ESCHEW feminological obfuscation!

THERE are three kinds of men, the handsome, the caring, and the majority.

WHEN a woman makes a fool of a man it is usually an improvement.

IF a woman does household chores for $200 a week, that's domestic science. If she does it for nothing, that's marriage.

A WOMAN who calls herself a bird deserves the worms she gets.

COMMON sense would save a significant number of marriages. If women used it there wouldn't be any.

THE men around here have obviously worked their way up from the bottom, and brought a lot of it with them.

IF you want a chick, go buy an egg.

WHAT would the world be without men? Free of crime, and full of fat, happy women.

AS the feminist said to the preacher:
   "So what's unusual about a man walking around and saying he was the Son of God?"

THERE are no damp patches when you are on top.

THE feminists were hailing a miracle birth. The baby had both, a dick AND a brain.

DO you know what you call that useless piece of skin on the end of a penis? A man!

A WOMAN who thinks the way to a man's heart is through his stomach is aiming a little too high.

SHE said her boyfriend wasn't a Sensitive New Age Guy, a SNAG. "No, he's more your Caring Understanding Nineties Type," she said.

WHEN all that's stiff is his socks, take the money and run.

A HARD man is good to find.

BETTER to have loved and lost than spend your whole damned life with him.

SHE said her boyfriend was like summer. He comes without warning and disappears for a year.

EVE was framed.

PENIS envy is a phallusy.

WHAT would you call a woman who always knows where her husband is? A widow!

100

MALE chauvinist pig's motto: Put Women's Libbers behind bras.

SUPPORT Women's Lib. Get out from under.

ADAM came first. But then, men always do.

AND once you've 'Adam, you 'Eve.

ADAM and EVEN.

A MAN wrapped up in himself makes a very small parcel.

GERMAN men live by the sweat of their fraus.

ONE man's Sunday lunch is one woman's Sunday gone.

A WOMAN'S lot is not a nappy one.

AND they lived happily after, someone else.

I USED to find him boring until I stopped listening.

MEN are like toilet seats. They are either vacant, engaged, or full of shit!

RUGBY players suffer from breast envy.

HOW can men take themselves seriously when they have got willies?

THE birth of Venus was a misconception.

A MAN who has lost 90% of his brain is called a widower.

Lesbians

A LESBIAN is a mannish depressive with delusions of gender.

IS a lesbian a pansy without a stalk?

WHAT do you call a lesbian with fat fingers? Well hung.

ARE you a practising lesbian? No. This is as good as I get.

Nymphomaniacs

A NYMPHOMANIAC is a woman who will make love the same day she has had her hair done.

SHE has a good job in the Nyphomaniacs Club. She examines prospective members.

THERE was once an English nymphomaniac. She simply had to have a man every six months.

IF it wasn't for orgasms our Noreen wouldn't know when to stop screwing.

THEY called her Elevator, because everybody in the building had been down on her.

HE approached the blonde and said: "Are you with anyone?"

She smiled and said, "Yes, I'm with anyone."

THE new blonde in the office is called Virginia. They called her Virgin for short, but not for long.

Gays

A HOMOSEXUAL is not a bloke who only does it at home.

TWO gays were arrested for riding a bisexual built for two.

OLD fairies never die. They simply blow away.

WE know a gay guy who is so ugly he has to go out with girls.

THE old actor said the queers in town were the ugliest he had ever encountered. "But then," he said, "buggers can't be choosers."

THE definition of an Aussie queer is a bloke who prefers girls to beer.

GAY pride is not a not a bunch of homosexual lions.

WITH gay marriages being recognised in America it follows that divorces will be recognised as gay abandon.

WHAT do you call a man who marries another man? A vicar.

IS camping loitering within tent?

TWO contented Irish gays were Thomas Fitzpatrick and Patrick Fitzthomas.

A NEW gay club in the Italian quarter is called Innuendo.

A NEW card game at the Gay Club is called camp poker. Queens are wild and straights don't count.

GAY sex is better
  Than bi-sex or hetter.

WHY are there so many queers in the British aristocracy? Have you seen their women?

I'LL be buggered if I'll join the British Conservative Party.

CECIL said it was true. Your entire life flashes before your eyes when you are gone down on for the third time.

DAISIES of the world unite. You have nothing to lose but your chains.

DID you hear about the gay tattoo artist who had designs on several sailors?

DID you hear about the girl whose bloke didn't drink, didn't swear and never made a pass at her? He also made his own dresses.

CECIL got a parking ticket for being too fast in the parking lot. The cop caught him at 69.

AN alligator walked into a men's wear shop.
    "Do you have any shirts with little faggots on the pocket?" he said.

THERE was an airline steward whose colleagues considered him a sexual pervert. He went out with women.

IF horse racing is the sport of kings, drag racing is the sport of queens.

HOW did it feel when you first discovered you were a homosexual? It was quite a blow.

WHEN two judges found they were gay they decided to try each other.

TWO words that will clear the gent's room, even at the interval break at the theatre.
    "N-i-i-ice dick!"

THE old prisoner confided to the warder that he thought his cell mate was becoming a queer. "He shuts his eyes when I kiss him goodnight," he explained.

THEY were leaning on the bar. "Have you ever slept with a gay?"
    "Certainly not. But I once slept with a bloke who had."

THE Greek soldier re-enlisted because he didn't want to leave his mate's behind.

THEN there was the Scottish gay, Ben Doon. He was found in the bush with nothing but an old Mackintosh on him.

IN the days of the Roman Empire many Romans thought that sex was a pain in the arse.

WHY are there so many gays in Italy? If you were brought up with so many ugly women what else could you be?

TWO fellows in a gay bar had a misunderstanding. They went outside and exchanged blows.

GOD save the Queens.

"HAVE Gums, Will Travel" - Prairie Fairy.

NIGEL was ready for the Gay Mardi Gras. He wanted to eat, drink and be Mary.

A GAY masochist is a sucker for punishment.

AS a football coach Cecil was in great demand by teams who wanted to know how to win by coming from behind.

GAY liberation is a pain in the arse.

Wankers

AT least a wanker is an owner operator.

HE was a whimsical masturbator with an off-beat sense of humour.

HE was such a wanker he used to fake orgasms during masturbation.

THERE is a big difference between wanking and clogs. You can hear yourself coming in clogs.

MASTURBATION is copulation without representation.

WHAT'S the difference between an egg and a wank? You can't beat a wank.

HE was such a conceited wanker he would call out his own name and come.

PRACTICE artificial insemination. Keep your hand in.

BOYCOTT symphony orchestras. Play with yourself.

WHY is masturbation better than intercourse?
  Because you know who you are dealing with.
  Because you don't have to buy flowers.
  Because you know when you've had enough.
  Because you don't have to be polite.
  Because you don't have to make conversation.
  Because you don't have to look your best.
  Because you meet a better class of person.
  Because it is with someone you love.

WANKING is very much like playing Bridge. If you've got a good hand you don't need a partner.

LOVERS may celebrate Valentine's Day, but wankers celebrate Palm Sunday.

TO argue with a crowd is mass debating.

AS the reformed wanker said: "I haven't been feeling myself lately."

HE confessed that he did it each night out of habit. "Then it's a habit you'll have to shake," said the priest.

MASTURBATION is a waste of fucking time.

Flashers

FLASHER'S motto: Grin and bare it.

FLASHER'S theme song: Whistle while you lurk.

IT was Fred the Flasher's most embarrassing experience. A woman charged him before the Small Claims Tribunal.

THE sign hanging on the lowest button of his overcoat read: "Next showing, 4pm."

WHEN Fred the Flasher was arrested in the car park he pointed to the council sign which said: "Pay and Display."

6
The Church and
Things Ecclesiastic

Religion

IN the world of one-liners nothing is sacred, least of all the sermons from the pulpit. "I don't mind them continually looking at their watches," said the vicar, "it's when they shake them to check if they are still going that pisses me off."

DO unto others before the bastards do it to you.

IT'S hard to believe the Darwin theory that only the fit have survived.

RELIGION is learning how to break the Fall.

MOSES couldn't believe it. He went back to God. "Tell me again. The Arabs get the oil and we get the end cut off our what?"

EVERYONE wants to go to heaven, but no one wants to die.

GOD is alive and well and working on a much less ambitious project.

HOW can we be sure God is dead when we can't be certain about Elvis?

PEOPLE are divided into two groups, the righteous and the sinful. And it is the righteous that do the dividing.

FRED doesn't go to church so much since he became a Seventh Day Absentist.

THE parishioner had reached the age where his regular five dollars on the collection plate was not so much a contribution as an investment.

IF all the people who slept in church were laid end to end they would be a lot more comfortable.

THE lamb and the lion will lie down together when the lamb hasn't anything the lion wants.

THE problem with most church congregations is the number of souls outnumbered by the number of heels.

OUR church welcomes all denominations; fives, tens, even fifties.

BECOME an agnostic. Worship the Agnos.

THE Creation was just a trial run.

WHAT do you say when you meet God and he sneezes?

HOW come the Madonna and Child had time to pose for all those paintings?

MY girlfriend wears a biblical dress, low and behold.

LET him among us to run the fastest cast the first stone.

THE meek shall inherit the earth. So long as nobody objects.

THE meek had a meeting today and decided they don't want to inherit the earth.

AS the Buddhist said to the priest: "I'm afraid my Carma has run over your Dogma."

SALMAN Rushdie's latest book is called Buddha Knew Bugger-All.

WAS Jesus the original pin-up?

GO to church on Sunday and avoid the Christmas rush.

A GENEROUS parishioner donated a loud-speaker for the church, in memory of his wife.

ADAM turned over a new leaf when he met Eve.

IN the beginning, the word was aardvark.

AVE Maria. Thanks, don't mind if I do.

REINCARNATION is a pleasant surprise.

THE Queen had a baby and they fired a 21-gun salute. The nun had a baby and they fired the dirty old canon.

THE trouble with born-again Christians is that they are a worse pain in the neck the second time around.

RELIGION is man's attempt to communicate with the weather.

ESKIMOS are God's frozen people.

THE first commandment was when Adam told Eve to eat the apple.

THE fifth commandment is humour thy father and thy mother.

THE seventh commandment is thou shalt not admit adultery.

IF Jesus is the answer, what the hell was the question?

LOVE thy neighbour, regularly.

SUDDEN prayers make God jump.

CHASTITY is its own punishment.

MY mother-in-law converted me to religion. I never believed in hell until I met her.

THE chief said, "I don't like the look of the missionaries."
His wife said, "That's all right then, just eat the vegies."

OF course it was a certainty that Jesus was Jewish. He lived at home until he was 30, he went into his father's business, his mother thought he was divine, and he thought she was a virgin.

He certainly wasn't an Australian. Where would you find three wise men, and where would you find a virgin?

LITTLE Johnny said he loved the Christmas story, especially the bit about the three wise guys from the east and Mary's immaculate contraption.

THE vicar said, "Tell me, young man, who went to Mount Olive?"
    "Popeye," was the quick response.

JERUSALEM is just a stone's throw from Tel Aviv.

NOAH'S wife was called Joan of Ark.

LOT'S wife was a pillar of salt by day, but a ball of fire by night.

JESUS ate the last supper with the twelve opossums.

THE epistles were the wives of the apostles.

A CHRISTIAN can only have one wife. This is called monotony.

TONIGHT'S sermon: "What is Hell?" Come early and listen to our choir practice.

CHRISTMAS comes but once a year. Thank God I'm not a Christmas.

THE dyslexic woke in the middle of the night and wondered if indeed there was a Dog.

ORIGINAL sin was wrong from the start.

EVERY Easter a sign goes up in Izzy's pawnbroker shop: "Christ has risen, but our prices remain the same."

YOUNG Billie returned from his first time at church. He said the music and singing were good, but he didn't think much of the news.

AT the Ecumenical dinner the priest taunted the Rabbi by asking him when he would become liberal enough to eat some of the ham.

"At your wedding," replied the rabbi.

TOURISTS were being charged $50 for a ferry trip across the Sea of Galilee. "Why so much? questioned McTavish. He was told that Jesus walked on these waters.

"At these prices I'm not surprised," said Mac.

THE lie is an abomination to the Lord; but bloody helpful in getting out of trouble.

GOD made man before woman because he didn't want anyone looking over his shoulder telling him how to do it.

THE radio announcer was delighted to hear his son saying his prayers, concluding with: "And here again, dear Lord, are the headlines."

THE sign on the cathedral door: "This is the House of God and these are the Gates of Heaven." And in smaller print: "Closed between 6pm and 10am."

THE sign on the church said: "If you are tired of sin, come in." And added in lipstick: "If not, ring Dulcie, 041-2468".

Vicars and the ministry

THE best passage from a boring sermon is from the pulpit to the vestry.

THE vicar and his housekeeper caused a scandal when they found his vest in her pantry and her pants in his vestry.

HE was a consistent preacher. After each of his sermons there was a significant awakening.

DO Church of England ministers get their pleasures vicariously?

WHAT a preacher. His sermons were like water to a drowning man.

PREACHING on the sin of pride the vicar asked how many extroverts were in the congregation. The bloke in the front row said "I don't know about the rest, but I'm Anglican."

Atheists

ATHEISM is a non-prophet organisation.

THE Atheists organised a dial-a-prayer service. When you phone up, nobody answers.

AN atheist is a man with no invisible means of support.

Catholics

IT is hard to envisage the torture of a man giving up his sex life only to have people come in and tell him the highlights of theirs. But here we go.

SIN is so bad at our parish lately that the church has added an extra confessional box with a sign over the door: "Eight items or less."

PRIEST in confessional: "Are you ever troubled with improper thoughts?"
   "No. I quite like them."

LITTLE Patrick said priests know more than rabbis.
   "Yeah," said little Izaac, "That's because you tell them everything!"

THE Pope is not inflammable.

TWO priests in Rome were discussing the Pope when he drove past in his Popemobile.
   "Talk of the Devil," said one.

POPE John Paul is Innocent.

EASTER is cancelled, they've found the body.

SO is Christmas, they've found the father.

THE Virgin Mary looked glum: "I was hoping for a girl!"

OH Blessed Virgin we believe
  That thou without sin did conceive
  Please teach us then, thus believing
  How we can sin without conceiving.

THE Vatican has taken over the railways and called it the Transportus Coitus Interruptus.
  Everybody gets off one stop before their destination.

PEOPLE who use the rhythm method of contraception are usually called Parents.

MANY believe that the Pope's phone number is Vat 69.
  It's not. It's Et Cum Spirri 2-2-0.

IT was H.L. Mencken who said: "It is now lawful for Catholic women to avoid pregnancy by resorting to mathematics, but unlawful to resort to physics and chemistry."

MY uncle was a missionary who converted cannibals to Catholicism. On Fridays they only eat fishermen.

WE go to the Bingo nights organised by the Catholic Church. The priest calls the numbers in Latin so the Protestants can't win.

SISTER Therese always slept with her clothes on. She just couldn't get out of the habit.

HELP a nun kick the habit.

A NUN who walks in her sleep is called a Roamin' Catholic.

MONKS do it out of habit.
   While nuns were once novices at it.

BECOME a nun and feel superior.

FEEL superior and fondle a nun.

ASKED why he left the church the altar boy said he couldn't stand the priest ramming religion down his throat.

SHOULD priests marry? Only if they love each other.

THE Pope's advisers said he should have a better image with the younger generation so they changed his name to Pope John Paul George and Ringo.

EXTREME unction is the last word.

Confesssion

YOU know your life is really dull when it comes to the end of the week and you've got nothing to confess.

7
Politics and Nationalities

Politics

PERHAPS politics is summarised by an incident from real life when a protege of Winston Churchill's sat on the front bench for the first time and looked across the House and said: "So, that's the enemy." Churchill corrected him. "No. That's the Opposition my boy. The enemy is behind you."

THE best way to succeed in politics is to find a crowd that's going somewhere and get in front of them.

TO be a leader you need a lot of people dumb enough to follow you.

A CONSERVATIVE is someone who believes that nothing should be done for the first time.

A CONSERVATIVE admires radicals a century after they are dead.

THE Conservative Party stands for innovation, progress and new ideas; but not yet.

SOME people believe in law and order, if they can lay down the law and give the orders.

THERE are some people who laugh at claims by hair restorers, yet believe election promises.

WHERE you stand depends on where you sit. Where you sit depends on who you know.

UNDER communism it's "dog eat dog". Under capitalism it is the reverse.

IN a democracy you can say what you think without thinking.

THE less a government costs, the more it's worth.

A CANDIDATE who leaves your party is a renegade, one who joins yours is a convert.

ELECTIONS consist of two sides and a fence.

WHY is there just one Monopolies Commission?

"I ADMIRE the straightforward way in which my opponent dodges the issue."

I DON'T support any organised party. I vote Labour.

LOOKING at the two candidates makes you grateful that only one can be elected.

WHY spend money tracing your family tree? Go into politics and have your opponents do it for you.

NOTHING is so admirable in politics as a short memory.

A FOOL and his money are soon elected.

GOVT is a four letter word.

THE government seems to believe that there's a taxpayer born every minute.

THE Prime Minister was asked if he had heard the latest political jokes.
"Heard them?" he said. "I work with the bludgers."

ONE politician said he wouldn't mind a bit if women were in power. The other said he wouldn't mind a bit, and he didn't give a stuff who was in power.

IF the government is getting up your nose, then picket.

POLITICIANS divide their time between running for office and running for cover. And passing the buck or passing the doe.

WHEN the politicians run it's the taxpayers who sweat.

THE explanation for any political stuff-up will be made by the deputy, or a stand-in inversely proportional down the ladder to the seriousness of the disaster.

PROGRESS may have been alright once, but it went on for too long.

NEO-NAZISM is a National Affront.

WHAT'S behind the National Front?

KARL Marx's grave is a communist plot.

I WISH he'd shut up about his silent majority.

FREE speech now! Abolish phone bills.

HANG extremists!

HE said he had half a mind to join the National Front.

NATIONALISE crime. Make sure it doesn't pay.

GUY Fawkes. Where are you when we need you?

NERO was a nervous Rex.

IF you feel strongly about graffiti, sign a partition.

GRAFFITI is the revenge of the inarticulate proletariate.

FIGHTING for peace is like fucking for virginity.

REMEMBER the golden rule: Those with the gold rule.

REPEAL the banana.

THE most useful Tory is a Lava.

122

GROUCHO was a Marxist.

WHEN a politician says a meeting was meaningful, it means that it was meaningless.

NEVER believe anything about a politician, until he has made an official denial.

WHY is it that the only people who know how to run the country are driving cabs or cutting hair?

IT has just been revealed that the Prime Minister was a test tube baby. Evidently nobody gave a fuck for him then either.

POLITICIANS are people who have to mind their appease and accuse.

ONE thing about our local MP. He's an honest politician. When he's bought he stays bought.

WHAT do you need when you have a politician up to his neck in concrete?
    More concrete.

THE politician went to Harley St, London, for a dick transplant. It rejected him.

COME to think of it, there is no difference between politicians and bull sperm. Only one in a thousand actually work.

AT the political rally the heckler yelled:
    "Clinton should be bloody well hung!"
    Hilary jumped up: "He is, he is."

THE State's health system is so run down that the Pregnancy Test Service now has a ten-month waiting list.

EAT figs and prunes and start a movement.

MAKE your MP work. Don't re-elect him.

DON'T vote. It only encourages the bastards.

IF you must vote, vote for the candidate who will do the least harm.

WHEN the presidential car containing four members of the cabinet was bombed it was a terrible waste. The car could have seated six.

A RECESSION is when your neighbour loses his job. A depression is when you lose your job. A recovery is when (the current Prime Minister) loses his job.

Nationalities

NATIONALISM is always a reason to be politically incorrect with a spray of one-liners. And don't forget, nationalism jokes are interchangeable. Just swap "Murphy" for "McTavish" or the mob you want to prod for taking themselves too seriously.

FRED protested when the doctor said he needed some shots against malaria. "No way," he said, "What have the Malarians ever done to me?"

THEY can't make ice cubes in Malaria anymore. The inventor died and took the recipe with him.

RACIAL prejudice is a pigment of the imagination.

IF God hadn't meant us to be racially prejudiced he would have made us all the same colour.

ETHNICS I don't mind. It's all these bloody foreigners that piss me off.

THE advantage of speaking another language is that you can talk behind someone's back right in front of their face.

GYPSIES are best at predicting the future because their fathers had crystal balls.

IT was an Irishman who invented the toilet seat. And a Scot who figured out how to put a hole in it.

Australians

A WELL-BALANCED Aussie is one with a chip on both shoulders.

THE difference between an Australian wedding and an Australian funeral is one less drunk.

AUSTRALIAN men suffer from premature ejaculation because they can't wait long enough to get down the pub and boast to their mates.

THEY give their dicks names because they don't want a stranger making 99 per cent of their decisions for them.

IN the beginning God made heaven and earth. Tasmania was an offcut.

HOW do you make an Aussie laugh on Monday morning? Tell him a joke on Friday night.

AFTER the Irish built a bridge across the Nullabour they found groups of Australians fishing from it.

WHAT is an Aussie lover's idea of foreplay?
   "HEY Cheryl. Wake up!"

WHAT is a Tasmanian's idea of foreplay.
   "Hey Mum. Wake up!

QUEENSLANDERS drink Four-X because it's the only beer they can spell.

"HEY Mum," he said as he rushed in from school. "I've got the biggest dick in grade five."
   "Well so you should. You will be 21 next August."

AUSSIES don't sign on for work, they sign the visitor's book.

WHAT do you call an Aussie with half a brain? Gifted.

HOW can you tell when an Aussie is formally dressed? He's wearing black thongs.

HOW do you make an AUSSIE LAUGH on MONDAY morning?

Tell him a JOKE on FRIDAY night

slap slap

HOW many Australian men does it take to lower a toilet seat? None. They've never tried it before.

A FORWARD thinking Aussie is the one who buys two slabs of beer instead of one.

WHAT is a typical Aussie's seven-course meal? A six-pack and a pie.

HAVE you heard about the Aussie punter who won $100 on the Melbourne Cup but lost $500 on the replay?

THE reason Aussies piss in the garden at parties is because there is always somebody throwing up in the toilet.

Arabs

A QUEER Arab is one who speaks with tongue in sheik.

EGYPTIAN girls who forget to take the pill are called Mummies.

WHAT do Arabs do on Saturday nights? Sit beneath palm trees and eat their dates.

WHAT is gross stupidity? 144 Iranians.

WHAT do you call an Iranian who practices birth control? A humanitarian.

YOU can't get a drink in Saudi Arabia, but you can get stoned anytime.

AYATOLLAH Khomeini is a Shiite.

Chinese

ACUPUNCTURE fees in China are so cheap it is called pin money.

THE estate agent said it was not the right location for a Chinese restaurant. He said: "They'd be flogging a dead horse."

THERE is a Chinese-Jewish restaurant in our neighbourhood. It's called Ghengis Cohen.

SAID the Chinese maid when she received her marriage licence: "It won't be wrong now."

CHINESE Proverb: Man who goes to bed with sex problem on mind wakes up with solution in hand.

CUSTOMER in Chinese cafe says: "This chicken is bloody rubbery!"
    Chinese proprietor replies: "Thank you plerry much."

Dutch

THE brave Dutch lad stuck his finger in the dyke.
    And she punched the bejeezus out of him.

WE know a Dutch wanker who always wore clogs so that he could hear himself coming.

English

YOU can tell a Pommie, but you can't tell him much.

DID you know the population of London is denser than Ireland and Wales put together?

WHEN does a Pommie become a Briton? When he marries your daughter.

BRITONS have an infinite capacity for churning themselves up into a terrific calmness.

AN Englishman and his wife finally achieved sexual compatibility for the first time. They both had a headache.

THE Lord of the Manor asserts that a wife made-to-order can't hold a candle to one ready maid.

WHY do British Bulldogs have flat faces?
   From chasing parked cars.

HOW do you save a Pommie from drowning?
   Shoot the bastard before he hits the water.

HOW do you get a Pommie out of the bath? Put water in it.

LEGEND has is that there was once an English nymphomaniac who had to have it every six months.

THE English football team was examined by a medical panel and pronouced fit for FA.

THE king fell madly in love with the court jester and from then on was always at his wit's end.

WHY is British beer like making love in a canoe? They are both fucking close to water.

French

A FRENCHMAN is a man who kisses other men on the cheeks and girls on all fours.

FRENCH girls are good at holding their liquor.
 "First, get ze good grip on 'ees ears," said Fifi.

THE best time to visit Paris is between your 18th and 25th birthdays.

FRENCH kissing is like a toothpick. It's good either end.

A FRENCH Square Dance is a Go Down Hoedown.

THERE will never be a French astronaut. Who ever heard of a Frenchman going up?

THE French groom was so exhausted by the wedding celebrations he fell asleep the moment his feet hit the pillow.

THE difference between a madam and a mademoiselle is a monsieur.

THE difference between French women and those in the rest of the world is simple: All women know what men like, but the French girl doesn't mind.

IN fact, a French girl went to live in London for a time, but she missed her native tongue.

Germans

THE German was so naive he thought Einstein was a single glass of beer.

A LAZY German lives by the sweat of his frau.

IT'S odd that the German police have been unable to catch the Nazis, especially as they were so efficient when they were the Nazis.

AS the Lufthansa captain announced: "You vill now fasten your safety belts. Und I just vant to hear one click; not clickety clickety click."

HANS always thought mine shaft was English for his donger.

Irish

THE Irish section needs an introduction of its own, and perhaps Irish logic can be best explained by this little twist on Gaelic one-liners:

THE neighbours gathered around the deceased Murphy. "He looks so tanned," said one. "The holiday must have done him the world of good."

"And he looks so calm and serene," said another.

"That's because he died in his sleep and doesn't know he's dead," said widow Murphy. "When he wakes up I'm sure the shock will kill him.

"And where is he being buried?"

"St Patrick's."

"Oh, so am I if the Good Lord spares me."

IF my husband was alive next Friday he'd be dead a year.

MURPHY said" Where's my fork and knife?"
   O'Reilly said: "It's in the fork 'n drawer."

DID you hear about the Irish thief who broke into the Collingwood Football Club's trophy room?

DID you hear about the Irishman who locked his keys in his car? It took him two hours to get his wife and kids out.

SIGN in an Irish pub: "If this is your first visit to Ireland you're welcome to it."

SIGN in the same pub: "If you have come in here to forget, please pay in advance."

IRISH publican: "Sorry gents. The pub won't be open for an hour, but would you like to come in and have a drink while you're waiting?"

IRISH logic: "I'm thin, and Murphy's thin, but O'Reilly is thinner than both of us put together."

"OFF to school now," said Mrs O'Grady to her kids. "And don't talk to strangers unless you know them."

"I hope ta God the doctor finds something wrong with me because I'd hate to feel like this if I was well."

WE have just heard of an Irish scientist who has invented a cure for which there is no known disease.

MURPHY to O'Toole: "If you can guess how many pups I've got in this sack you can have both of them."

WHEN Brigid told her mother she was pregnant the response was: "Begorrah. Are you sure it's yours?"

THE Irish Mafia will make you an offer you can't understand.

PADDY caused a sensation the day he streaked through the nudist camp.

WHERE do the Irish keep their armies? Up their sleevies.

WHY do Irishmen wear two condoms? To be sure, to be sure.

MURPHY hates daylight saving. He gets his early morning erection on the 8.30 train to the office.

HOW do the Irish count bank notes?
"One, two tri, four, foive, another, another, another ....!"

THE Irish call their basic currency the punt, because it rhymes with bank manager.

IRISH loan sharks lend money at ridiculous rates, then skip town.

THERE was a riot in an Irish prison and the governor told the warders to evict the trouble-makers.

PADDY thought oral sex was just talking about it.

WHY is semen white and urine yellow? So that an Irishman can tell if he is coming or going.

CLEANLINESS is next to Godliness.But only in the Irish dictionary.

FLANNIGAN joined Alcoholics Unanimous. "There are no arguments," he explained.

THE Irish ventriloquist was so bad his lips were moving when he wasn't saying anything.

THERE was a power failure in a Dublin department store. Thousands of shoppers were stranded on the escalators for hours.

"TERESA has just had twins," roared Murphy angrily. "Wait till I get my hands on the other fellow."

TERESA said: "I don't t'ink my husband has been completely faithful to me. My last child doesn't resemble him in th' least."

THE Irish maiden's prayer: "And now Dear Lord, please have Murphy on me."

PADDY: "Hey Shaun, what's Mick's surname?"
   Shaun: "Mick who?"

MURPHY and his bride sat up all night waiting for their sexual relations to arrive.

HOW do you sink an Irish submarine? Knock on the hatch.

SHAMUS the Irish gourmet says, contrary to culinary practice one shouldn't drink wine with fish. "Eventually the fish become very abusive," he said.

FLAHERTY says women have only themselves to blame for all the lying men do. "They never stop asking questions," he said.

SHAMUS said his wife was a kleptomaniac, but her sister is worse. "She walks out of stores backwards and leaves things on the counter."

THEN there was the Irish cat. It shit in the garden and then buried itself.

AND the Irish Dingo that went into the Alice Springs botanic gardens and ate all the azaleas.

Italians

Is an IQ of 105 considered high?
   Yes. For ten Italians.

LUIGI said he was damn lucky. He's got a wife and a transistor, and they both work.

Why does an Italian have a hole in his pocket?
  So he can count to six.

ALL Italian boys grow moustaches, so that they can look like their mums.

THE Mafia moll dumped her boyfriend when she learned he was just a finger man.

RECTAL thermometers are banned in Italy.
  They found they cause too much brain damage.

HOW do Italian men propose to their girlfriends?
  "You're gonna have a what?"

DID you hear about the Italian who stayed up all night studying for his urine test?

WHEN the Italian girl had sex in the back seat of a hire car she said: "It'sa Herts."

SIGN on Luigi's new house: "Costa Plenti."

WHAT is a specimen?
  An Italian astronaut.

WHAT'S the national bird of Italy?
  The stool pigeon.

IN Sicily a tourist was arrested for failing to bribe a police officer.

WHAT do you call Sophia Loren?
A pizza arse.

BIGOTRY is a tall redwood, while a bigamist is a thick fog over Rome.
And an innuendo is an Italian suppository.

IN America an Italian is really a Mexican with a job.

Japanese

WHEN Japanese men have erections, they vote.

JAPANESE cunnilingus is constluctive cliticism.

A JAPANESE orgasm is a gland finale.

A PELVIC examination in Japan is a nookie lookie.

LACKA-NOOKIE is one of Japan's most dreaded diseases.

SACKA-NOOKIE is Japanese for bloomers.

THE Japanese call girl went broke.
Nobody had a yen for her.

THE Japanese firm making vibrators is Genital Electric.

AND there is a new Japanese camera.
When you trip the shutter it goes "crick".

WE know a bloke who is half Japanese and half Black.
Every December 7 he attacks Pearl Bailey.

Jewish

THE Jews are the most confident race in the world.
   They cut the end off their dick before they know
how long it will grow.

IZZY said it was such a shock when he got circumcised he couldn't walk for 18 months.

WHAT do you call an uncircumcised Jewish baby?
   A girl.

THE Talmudic scholar wondered how it could possibly be a Christian world when the sun was named Sol.

ONE of the greatest Jewish leaders in Scotland was Rabbi Burns.

WHAT'S six inches long, has a bald head and drives Jewish women wild?
   An American one hundred dollar bill.

THE difference between an Italian woman and a Jewish woman is that one fakes orgasms and has real diamonds.

A CATCH 22 situation for a Jew is free pork.

OF all the pornographic movies Jewish films are the worst; 5 minutes of sex and 95 minutes of guilt.

THERE was a Jewish kamikaze pilot.
He crashed his plane into his brother's scrap metal yard.

THE first Jewish astronaut was Nose Cohen.

"PAPPA," said the lad. "What's Yiddish for a hundred per cent?"

"Izzy, my son, a hundred per cent is Yiddish."

A JEWISH nymphomaniac is a woman who allows her husband to make love to her after she has been to the hairdresser.

WHY does a Jewish wife close her eyes while having sex?

God forbid she should see her husband having a good time.

WHY do Jewish women wear two-piece bathers?

To separate the milk from the meat.

IZZY Cohen hires midgets as waiters because it makes his sandwiches look bigger.

WHEN Mrs Fink walked out without her change Izzy tried to call her back by banging on the shop window with a sponge.

WHEN asked to name the four seasons Izzy replied:

"I only know two. Busy and slack."

WE know a rabbi who keeps a scrapbook of all his clippings.

LITTLE Izzy came home from school with a note: "Izzy is too easily distracted. He never concentrates."

So they sent him to a concentration camp.

New Zealanders

TOBY had a little lamb
  His case comes up next Friday.

WHAT'S long, hard and fucks New Zealanders?
  Grade Three.

A KIWI farmer was counting his sheep.
  "301, 302, 303, 304, hello darling, 306, 307 ..."

THREE couples went into a restaurant in Auckland and asked for a table for sex.
  "And three pillows," they added.

WHY do New Zealanders have sex with sheep on the edge of cliffs?
  Because they push back harder.

Russians

LITTLE Red Riding Hood is a Russian contraceptive.

WHAT do you call an attractive woman in Russia?
  A tourist.

Scots

THE reason Scots have blisters on their dicks is because they are such tight-fisted wankers.

JOCK McPerv was so mean he used to reverse charge his obscene telephone calls.

WHAT do Scotsmen do with their old condoms?
  They keep shagging with them.

WHEN Jock had a vasectomy he asked the doctor if he was entitled to severance pay.

HOW does a Scot take a bubble bath?
  He has baked beans for supper the night before.

"IS anything worn under that kilt?"
  "Nay lass. Everything is in perfect working order."

SCOTS wear kilts because they haven't any pockets.

DID you hear about the Scot who found a crutch?
  He broke his wife's leg.

AS McTavish scolded his son: "Don't wear your glasses unless your are looking at something important."

A SCOTTISH gentleman is one who gets out of the bath to piss in the sink.

START of a Scottish recipe:
  First borrow three eggs.

WHEN McTavish took his new girl friend out in a taxi she was so lovely he could hardly keep his eyes off the meter.

A TRUE Scot never sends his pyjamas to the laundry unless he has a pair of socks stuffed in the pocket.

DO you know what McTavish did with his first fifty cent piece?
   Married her.

THE Scotsman gave the waiter a tip.
   It didn't even run a place.

THEN there's the Scot who drinks Scotch and Horlicks. When it is his turn to shout he is fast asleep.

A SCOTSMAN can drink any given amount.

THREE Scots were in church one Sunday when the collection plate came their way. One fainted and the other two carried him out.

DOWN at the Edinburgh Arms the worst drunk at the bar is always Duncan Disorderly.

HAPPY hour at the Caledonian is from 6pm to 6.30pm.

A SCOTSMAN has a sense of humour because it's a gift.

A SCOTTISH hotel is an establishment where they pinch the towels off the guests.

Turks

WHEN the sultan entered his harem unexpectedly his wives let out a terrified sheik.

THE sultan had ten wives.
   Nine of them had it pretty soft.

Welsh

WHY do the Welsh always sing?
Because they have no locks on the dunny doors.

WHAT do you call a Welsh vasectomist?
Dai Abollickal.

WHAT do you get if you cross a Welshman with a boomerang?
A nasty smell you can't get rid of.

8
Character Assassination

Insults

"GO and stick your head up a dead bear's bum" is an *effective means of ending a conversation and probably ending the relationship altogether. For those who like to be a tad more subtle here's a list of more gentle insults.*

I WAS going to call you a bastard, but you're too ugly to be a love child.

I'M telling you straight. Deep down you're shallow!

THEY tell me scientists are trying to build the perfect idiot and they're using you for the model?

YOU are the kind of chap who has plenty to be modest about.

YOU are someone who can bring a feeling of happiness and laughter into a room, simply by leaving it.

IF there is ever a price on your head, take it.

I NEVER forget a face, but in your case I'll make an exception.

YOU won't find him in "Who's Who," but you will find him in "What's That?"

I'M not saying you're stupid, but when I looked up nincompoop in the dictionary, there was your picture.

YOU have often been described as a pain in the neck, but I have a much lower opinion of you.

YOU can brighten up the room just by leaving it.

YOU are a man who brings happiness whenever you go.

SHE was never popular. One day a man took her out and left her there.

SHE has a tongue that jaywalks over every conversation.

SHE'S Vogue on the outside and vague on the inside.

HE told her he was a self-made man.
   She said she would accept that as an apology.

HE was so dumb it was written all over his face. And even then it was spelt wrong.

AUTOMATION will never replace Monty. They haven't come up with a machine that is absolutely useless.

MONTY is the original reason for birth control and his family have been trying to make it restrospective.

YOU will have to excuse him. He is going through a nonentity crisis.

NEXT time you pass my house I'd appreciate it.

DON'T move. I want to forget you exactly as you are.

SHE'S not such a bad person, until you get to know her.

HE'S a self-made man who obviously gave the job to the lowest bidder.

YOU claim to have an open mind. It's more like a vacant block.

WHAT a couple. They remind me of psychotherapy.
  And he's therapy.

HE reminds me of a beer bottle. Empty from the neck up.

HIS mouth is so big he can whisper in his own ear.

HE works as a tout for a doctor. He goes around making people sick.

HE is the biggest bull artist since Picasso.

HE'S not very amusing. He wouldn't even entertain a doubt.

HE is something like a sausage,
   Very smooth upon the skin,
   But you can never tell exactly,
   How much hog there is within.

HE'S useless. He has absolutely nothing. And if you
will excuse me for saying so he has very little of that.

HE'S as useless as half a scissors.

HE'S as useless as an ash tray on a motorbike.

HE is as useless as a one-legged man in an arse-kick-
ing contest.

HE is so mean that if he paid you a compliment he
would ask for a receipt.

HE will never pick up the bill. You've really got to
hand it to him.

CAN I have this dance?
   Sure, if you can find someone to dance with.

"COULD I have the last dance?" he said.
   "You've just had it," she replied.

"IF you were my husband I would give you poison."
   "If I was your husband I'd take it."

HE was the kind of person Dr Spooner would have
called a shining wit.

YOU wouldn't worry what people think of you if you knew how seldom they do.

I HAVE never supported abortion until now, and in your case I would make it restrospective.

THE only difference between you and a shopping trolley is that the trolley has a mind of its own.

SHE goes out with men by the score. And they all do.

The only difference between her and the Titanic is that we know how many went down on the Titanic.

THE only difference between you and a bucket of shit is the bucket.

WHEN the club bore asked him to play a round of golf he replied: "No thanks. If I want to play with a prick I will play with my own."

POMPOUS git at the gentleman's club told the waiter he would have his coffee like he has his women, hot, sweet and stirred up.
   "Black or white?" responded the waiter.

HIS mother would be most upset if she knew he was a journalist. She still thinks he is running dope from Bangkok.

TWICE already she has been asked to marry.
   Once by her mother and once by her father.

IF you think the service is bad, wait until you taste the food.

HE'D steal the harness off a nightmare.

SHE was so mean she used to heat the knives so the family would use less butter.

HE'S very broad-minded. He thinks of little else.

THEY were thicker than mourners at a brewer's wake.

IF I'd known she'd take offence so easily I would have entered her in the Grand National.

SHE might have eyes like two limpid pools, but she has a nose like a diving board.

SHE spent five hours at the beauty salon yesterday, just getting an estimate.

THAT girl has everything a man could want; muscles, hair on her chest, moustache, beard ...

SHE was only the horse trainer's daughter, but all the horse manure.

SHE was only a newsagent's daughter, but she loved her Daily Mail.

SHE was only a cab driver's daughter, but you sure auto meter.

SHE was only an antique dealer's daughter but she wouldn't allow much on the sofa.

SHE was only the sergeant's daughter but you should have seen her privates.

SHE was only a cricketer's daughter but she could take a full toss in the crease.

SHE can be outspoken, but I've never seen anyone do it yet.

HE is so argumentative he won't even eat food that agrees with him.

HE doesn't have a lot to say. Unfortunately you have to listen quite a while to find that out.

YOU are a man of few words. The trouble is you keep repeating them.

EVEN when he was a boy scout he was unreliable. He used to walk little old ladies halfway across the road.

HE is so arrogant he does crossword puzzles with a felt-tip pen.

HE had an ego bigger than the Outdoors.

I HOPE I die before her. I want to see Heaven before she improves it.

"YOUR scones," said the guest," were so lovely that I ate four."
   "Five, but who is counting," said the host.

Losers

HE is such a loser he was once knocked back by a prostitute who told him she had a headache.

HE once lent $10,000 to a mate for plastic surgery and now can't recognise him.

WHEN he was born he was such an ugly baby the doctor slapped his mother.

HE has always worked for charity. He has to. Nobody will pay him.

HIS life is so dull the only social outings he has to look forward to are regular visits to the dentist.

THE last time he was in hospital he got Get Well cards from all the nurses.

HE applied to join the Lonely Hearts Club, but they wrote back and said they were not that lonely.

HE was an only child, and he still wasn't his mother's favourite.

HE has willed his body to science, and science is contesting the will.

HE has just been served a paternity suit by lawyers acting for his children.

WHEN they circumcised him they threw the wrong bit away.

HE'S such a loser he was once shipwrecked on an island with his own wife.

HE once spent a fortune on deodorants before he realised that people didn't like him anyway.

Dumb

HE was so dumb he was three bricks short of a load, not the full two-bob and three sandwiches short of a picnic.

SHE is so dumb she thinks an aperitif is a set of dentures.

HE thinks an alter ego is a conceited priest.

SHE thinks intercourse is a ticket to the races.

HE thinks Vat 69 is the Pope's phone number.

SHE thinks the Union Jack is something you get at the trades hall.

HE thinks hypocrisy was a Greek philosopher.

SHE thinks a bigamist is a thick Italian fog.

HE thinks fidelity is unadultered boredom.

SHE thought Good Friday did Robinson Crusoe's housework.

HE thinks Robinson Crusoe was a world famous tenor.

SHE thinks a Norwegian fjord is a Scandinavian car.

HE thinks manual labour is a Spanish waiter.

SHE thinks Chou-en-lai is Chinese for breakfast in bed.

HE thinks a brassiere is something you warm your hands on.

SHE thought an au pair was a living bra.

HE thinks polyunsaturated is a parrot in a raincoat

SHE thinks awestruck is being hit by a paddle.

HE thinks a bulletin is a can of pressed beef.

SHE thinks climate is the only thing you can do with a ladder.

HE thinks hyacinth is a greeting for anyone called Cynthia.

SHE thinks an optimist is a hope addict.

HE thinks odious is not very good poetry.

SHE thinks an operetta is a girl who works at the telephone exchange.

HE thinks Yoko Ono is Japanese for "One egg please."

SHE thinks a transistor is a nun in men's clothes.

HE thinks grammar is the woman who married grandpa.

SHE thinks Joan of Ark was Noah's wife.

HE thinks a lieutenant commander is the lieutenant's wife.

SHE thinks pregnant is the past tense of virgin.

HE thinks a polygon is a dead parrot.

SHE thinks the tooth fairy is a gay dentist.

HE thinks the landed gentry were tricked into marriage.

SHE thinks blue serge is a sad Russian.

HE thinks a cross section of the public are taxpayers.

SHE thinks a crowbar is where the girls hung out for a drink.

HE thought badminton was why the lamb tasted awful.

SHE thinks good housekeeping is the name of a magazine.

SHE thinks a penal colony is an all-male nudist camp.

HE thought Karl Marx was the brother of Chico and Harpo.

SHE thought Columbine was the wife of the guy who discovered America.

HE thought that where there is life there is opium.

SHE thought kosher was Jewish bacon.

HE thought myxomatosis was wiping out rabbis.

SHE thought a meadow lark was a frolic in a paddock.

HE thought vice versa was a rude poem.

SHE thought a metronome was a midget who worked on the Paris underground.

HE thought a teetotaller was the score-keeper at golf.

SHE thought ping pong balls was a Chinese sexual disease.

Jokes

"WHY a joke section?" I hear you all mutter. Well mainly because these one-liners don't fit in any other category and why miss them for want of a heading?

HUMOUR is to life what shock absorbers are to a car.

ONE of the best things you can have up your sleeve is a funny bone.

A COMEDIAN is too often the Goof that Relays the Olden Gag.

AN old comedian complained that he was always being told one of his own stories. A clear case of the tale dogging the wag.

THE only catch in telling a good story, is that it usually reminds the other bloke of a bad one.

THERE is nothing so hollow as laughing at the joke you were just about to tell yourself.

"I'VE got a million jokes," he said.
    "Then why did you tell us that one," they said.

HE who laughs last doesn't get the joke.

"HAVE you heard my last joke?
    "I hope so."

THE reason there is so much humour in the world is that there are so many people who take themselves seriously.

COMEDIANS say people don't like new jokes, but how would they know?

A COMEDIAN is someone who knows a good joke when he steals one.

"SO your sister makes up jokes. Is she a humourist?"
    "No. She works in a beauty salon."

MY wife knows all my jokes backwards. And that's how she tells them.

I TOLD my wife she didn't have a sense of humour.
  "I married you didn't I?" she replied.

HE said he finally got his boss to fall about laughing.
  Did he tell him a joke?
  No. He asked for a raise.

SHOW me a bloke who can laugh when everything goes wrong and I'll show you an idiot.

BLOKE goes into a fish shop and says: "Piece of flake and a dollar's worth of chips, twice."
  "Okay, okay," said Murphy, "Oi heard ya the first time."

9
Snobs and the Social Graces

Society

ALMOST every society is a zoo, with a few social lions, a few queer birds, a couple of white elephants, and a number who insist on making monkeys of themselves with etiquette and social graces.

SOCIETY is where people spend money they haven't got to buy things they don't need to impress people they don't like.

DON'T try to keep up with the Joneses. It's cheaper to drag them down to your level.

A SNOB is a bloke who invents ancestors who would disown him if they were real.

I COULD hardly believe I was at this high class function. I was the only person there I hadn't heard of.

BREEDING isn't everything, but it is certainly a lot of fun.

ETIQUETTE can be, at the same time, a means of approaching people and staying clear of them.

IN a social situation, that which is the most difficult thing to do is usually the right thing to do.

A BIRD in the hand is bad table manners.

THERE are people whom one should like to shun but would not wish to be shunned by.

TACT is the ability to describe others as they see themselves.

YOU are ushered in according to your dress and shown out according to your brain.

FORMAL wear for Australians is care to ensure that one's thongs are the same colour.

BEHIND every successful man is the Joneses.

THE upper crust is just a lot of crumbs sticking together.

THE upper crust is just a few crumbs held together by a lot of loose dough.

YOU'RE only young once. That's all society can stand.

YOU can tell when a socialite's husband has just died. She's the one in the black tennis skirt.

A FRIEND is one who has the same enemies as you.

THERE is not much talk at parties, until one or two couples leave.

WHEN you know nothing but good about a person it is more fun to talk about someone else.

NOTHING makes you more intolerant of a noisy neighbourhood party than not being there.

THERE'S nothing worse than when the party gets sordid and boring, and you can't leave because you are the host and it's at your place.

IF guests overstay their welcome, then treat them as members of the family. They will soon leave.

THE bore is the one who insists on talking about himself when you want to talk about yourself.

WHEN two egoists meet it's a case of an I for an I.

A MIDDLE class family is one that lives in public like the rich do and in private like the poor do.

HIS family have been aristocrats for degenerations.

HE is a member of the effluent society; one of the stinking rich.

A GOOD host makes his guests feel at home, even though he wished they were.

HE had the manners of a gentleman. I knew they could not have belonged to him.

CHIVALRY is not dead, yet. If a teenage girl drops her book a teenage boy is likely to kick it over to her.

Drinkers and
Alcoholics Anonymous

LET'S face it, booze is a subject we all understand as most of us have a friend or an Uncle Monty who tipples, or gives the bottle a nudge.

AN alcoholic is a man who goes in to a topless bar for a drink.

MONTY is known as a light drinker. As soon as it's light he starts to drink.

MURPHY has joined Alcoholics Unanimous because he says there are never any arguments.

HI-FIDELITY is a drunk who always goes home to his wife.

THE man who goes into a bar optimistically, usually leaves misty optically.

BEGGARS can't be boozers.

GOING steady only means you've sobered up.

"WHAT would you like to drink to?"
  "What about three in the morning?"

WINE improves with age. The older I get the more I like it.

ANY port in a storm is better than no rum.

ALL too often a keen judge of whisky is also a merciless executioner.

ABSTINENCE is the thin edge of the pledge.

BEER will be my urination.

YOU can tell the town drunk by the rust on his fly.

DIGNITY is one thing that alcohol doesn't preserve.

MONTY has a serious drink problem. He can't afford it.

HE drinks to forget, but he's forgotten why.

HE may drink to forget, but you may notice he never forgets to drink.

HE believes the best way to pull himself out of trouble is with a cork screw.

AFTER three whiskies my wife turns into a disgusting beast. After a fourth I pass out altogether.

ONE reason elephants drink so much water is that nobody offers them anything else.

WHEN Murphy fainted in the pub they brought him to, then they brought him another two and he was once more his chirpy self.

MURPHY said he always knows when he has had too much. "I feel people walking on my hands," he said.

DRUNK to barman: "Has Paddy been in tonight?"
   "Yes."
   "Was I with him?"

THE doctor told him he would have to limit his drinking to one glass per day. He is now up to January 15, 2005.

HE said it was terrible beer they served in that pub and he would be glad when he's had enough.

BRUCE the boozer has finally given up drink for the sake of his wife and kidneys.

HE suffers from alcoholic constipation.
   He can't pass a pub.

HE suffers from alcoholic rheumatism.
   HE gets stiff in most joints.

HE said he always falls on the floor after one whisky. Usually it was the 15th.

DRUNKS' Law: Remember, you can't fall off the floor.

CUT out the middle man. Pour the beer down the toilet.

DRINKERS' motto: Conserve water, always dilute it.

FRED denied that smoking in bed caused his house to burn down.

"First, I don't smoke," he said, "second, the bed was on fire when I got into it."

MONTY says he will never forget the day he turned to the bottle as a substitute for women. He got his dick stuck in one.

SHE described her husband as a musical drunk: "He goes out fit as a fiddle and comes home as tight as a drum."

I KNOW I'm drunk when I feel sophisticated and can't pronounce it.

"WHERE'S the nearest boozer?"
  "You're looking at him."

HE invented a new cocktail called Card Table. When you've had a couple your legs fold up under you.

HE called his latest cocktail Chook Juice. You lay where you drink it.

THERE'S nothing wrong with drinking like a fish so long as you drink what a fish drinks.

AVOID the Christmas rush. Drink now.

Pubs and life at the local

THINGS are so tough at our local pub they have employed a chucker-in!

WE call our local pub the Stradivarius. Because it is a vile inn!

THE publican has introduced a fifty cent entrance fee. It's to keep out the riff-raff.

THE beer's so flat at our pub they serve it on a plate.

McTAVISH took the publican aside and told him how he could sell more beer.
   "Just fill the glasses up properly," he said.

MEN have two reasons for staying in the pub all night.
   Either they have no wives to go home to, or they have.

HE said he couldn't stay long: "The wife thinks I'm in the bath."

BLOKE went into a pub and had a ploughman's lunch.
   It got the ploughman really pissed off.

SHE sauntered up to the bar and said: "Mine's a Light."
   And they threw a bucket of water over her.

"GIVE me something long and cold," he said to the barmaid. "Sure," she replied, "take my husband."

LOOKING around nostalgically he said, "Ya know, it's two years since I've been in this bar."
   "Quit moaning," said the barmaid," I'm serving as fast as I can."

A VENTRILOQUIST asked the barmaid for a gottle of gear and then drank it without moving his lips.

THE punter asked if they served women in the bar.
   No. He was told to bring his own.

THE barman gave her a nasty look. She didn't need it.
   She already had one.

HE wanted to go to a topless bar.
   So they took him to the pub with no roof.

AT a city hotel a waiter was dismissed for having his thumb in the soup and a topless waitress was dismissed for two similar offences.

THERE was an argument at the topless bar when the president of the Beer Appreciators' Society complained that the beer was okay but his waitress was flat.

"THE flies are thick," said a drinker.
   "Well what would expect out here," said the barman, "educated ones?"

"DO you drink to excess?"
   "I drink to anything."

THEN there's the Scot who drinks Scotch and Horlicks. When it is his turn to shout he is fast asleep.

A SCOT pushes his way to the bar. "I've had an attack of the Yaws," he says to the barman.
   "What's Yaws?" he says.
   "Double whisky," says the canny Scot.

IT was the ultimate in singles bars. Girls had to show their IUDs to be admitted.

A BLOKE went in to the pub with a chequered flag and the barman said: "Now don't you start anything."

Clubs and Committees

THE reunion or the annual general meeting usually consists of mundane reports that could well do with an irreverant one-liner or two.

THE length of a progress report is inversely proportional to the amount of progress.

WE have all passed a lot of water under the bridge since we last met.

WE have a few apologies. Our treasurer can't get bail.

OUR president has slaved over a hot secretary on behalf of us all.

HE never leaves a turn unstoned.

HALF the members of most committees are hopeless layabouts while the other half do all the work, but with our committee it is completely the reverse.

THE Eleventh Commandment: Thou shalt not committee!

A COMMITTEE is 12 men doing the work of one.

THOSE most opposed to serving on the committee are usually made chairman.

A COMMITTEE is a cul-de-sac where good ideas are lured, then quietly strangled.

MANY a meeting starts at 8pm sharp and finishes at 10pm dull.

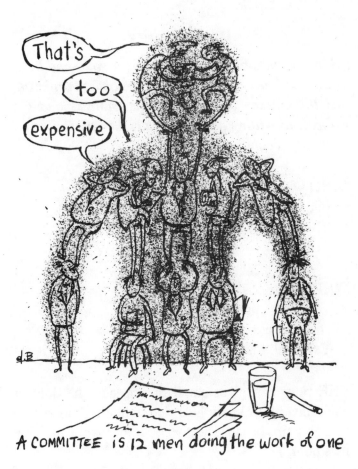

A COMMITTEE is 12 men doing the work of one

10
Dining Out

Restaurants

AS the restaurant writer put it: If the soup had been as warm as the wine and the wine as old as the chicken, and the chicken as tender as the waitress and the waitress as willing as the landlady then the inn could be highly recommended.

"AND what'll ya have?"
　　Said the waiter, idly picking his nose.
　　"I'll have two boiled eggs, ya bastard,
　　Ya can't put your fingers in those!"

WHEN the tip is hid,
　　'neath the edge of the plate,
　　The waitress knows
　　It's not all that great.

THE rich man gives small tips because he doesn't want anyone to know he's rich, while the poor man gives big tips because he doesn't want anyone to know he's poor.

IT was the most authentic Mexican restaurant I've been to. When the waiter brought me a glass of water he advised me not to drink it.

HE walked into the seafood restaurant and said: "Do you serve crabs here?"
  "We serve anyone. Take a seat."

"DO you have frogs legs?"
  "Of course."
  "Well hop over the counter and bring me some fags."

"Can you tell me the time?" asked a diner.
  "Sorry, mate," replied the waiter, "This is not my table."

THE topless waitress glared at the diner: "Will you stop staring at me," she said. "This is not my table."

SAID the wife to the husband: "I promised Rover we'd bring home a doggie bag, so do order something he likes."

HE saw a sign in a restaurant which said: "Watch Your Hat." So he did, and somebody stole his dinner.

THE coffee they serve is a special blend; some of yesterday's with today's.

"HEY, waiter this coffee tastes like mud."
  "Well it was ground just half an hour ago."

SHE was such a noisy eater three couples got up to dance when she started on her soup.

SIGN in a restaurant: "If you want to butt your cigarettes in the cup and saucer, let the waitress know and she can serve your coffee in the ashtray."

"I'LL have a crocodile sandwich, and make it snappy!"

Waiters

"WAITER, what's the best dish in the place?"
  "The blonde at table three, Sir."

WAITER: "How did you find the meat Sir?"
  "I just lifted a potato chip and there it was."

"WAITER, this plate is wet!"
  "That's you're soup, Sir."

"WAITER, this soup isn't fit for a pig."
  "I'll take it back and get some that is."

"WAITER, this soup tastes funny."
  "Well, start laughing."

"WAITER, what's this fly doing in my soup?"
  "Backstroke, I believe sir."

"WAITER, your thumb is on my steak."
  "Well, you wouldn't want it to drop on the floor again, would you?"

"WAITER, why does this chicken have one leg missing?"
  "It was in a fight."
  "Well, bring me the winner."

WAITER: "Will you have the pie, sir?"
  "Is it customary?"
  "No, it's apple."

ENGRAVED on the Maitre d's tombstone: "Bye and bye, God caught his eye."

IF you think the service is bad, wait until you taste the food.

"YOU haven't touched the fish," said the waiter.
  "Long time no sea," explained the diner.

"WAITER, this food is terrible, I demand to see the owner."
  "Sorry, Sir. He's out to lunch."

SOME waiters should visit the zoo and watch the turtles dashing about.

Home cooking

IF you like home cooking, you should have stayed home.

I MISS my wife's cooking, as often as I can.

EVERY morning I have coffee with two lumps; my wife and her mother.

MY wife is such a hopeless cook that Gourmet magazine tried to buy back her subscription.

MY wife cooks for fun. For food we go to restaurants.

ANY left-overs are given to the dog; who quickly gives them to the cat.

MY wife always throws out the left-overs. She should throw out the originals too.

THE best way to eat spinach is to fatten a chook with it then eat the chook.

WHERE'S there's smoke, there's toast.

MY wife uses the smoke detector as a timer.

11
Leisure

Sports

NEVER fall in love with a tennis player.
To them love means nothing.

A MEMORABLE over in test cricket began when the BBC commentator announced:
"The bowler's Holding, the batsman's Willy."

AT the club dance he explained to his partner: "I'm a little stiff from Badminton."
"I don't give a stuff where you come from," she replied, "just keep off my bloody feet."

SHE thought lacrosse was something you found in la church.

THE tipster said this horse would walk it in. It did, but all the others galloped.

MONTY used to be an all-round athlete.
Now, as you notice, he's just all-round.

THE English football team was examined by a medical panel and pronouced fit for FA.

THEY called it golf because all the other four-letter words were already taken.

FUNNY how man blames fate for all accidents, yet claims full responsibility for a hole in one.

FRED said during his last game of golf he stepped on a rake.
"They were the best two balls I hit all day!"

HER golf is improving. Yesterday she hit a ball in one.

NOW she has improved so much she misses the ball much closer than she used to.

SHE always wears two pair of pants to golf, in case she gets a hole in one.

A BELOW par golfer always takes two or three lumps with his tee.

"I GOT a set of clubs for my husband."
"Lucky you, what a swap!"

THE annual university boat race resulted in an exciting finish, but there was a dramtic moment when a blonde rushed through the crowd and kissed the cox of the winning crew.

Motoring

WE have it on good authority that the best thing that can be said about the advent of motoring is that it has virtually stamped out horse-stealing. And that is an excellent example of how to use an item from this book as an introduction.

YOU can always tell the happy motor cyclist by the insects on his teeth.

AN Irish pillion rider is called Pat on the back.

I CALL my car Flattery. It gets me nowhere.

HER driving is improving. Now when she parks it is only a short walk to the pavement.

HIS wife said: "Be an angel and let me drive."
   So he did, and now he is.

THE ideal combination on the road is to have the horse sense of the driver equal to the horse power of the car.

A BACK-SEAT driver never runs out of gas.

YOU can get some first-hand knowledge from a second-hand car.

I BOUGHT the car on hire payment; 20% down and the balance on receipt of regular threatening letters.

THE smoothest thing about a used car is the salesman.

IN words of one cylinder, you could have knocked me down with a fender.

HIS new car is so small the glove box only takes three fingers.

NOTHING makes your car run better than finding out how much money you need to buy a new one.

THE trouble with my car is the engine won't start and the payments won't stop.

ALWAYS try to drive so that your licence expires before you do.

I HAVE No-Fault car insurance. When I have an accident I just call the insurance company and they tell me it isn't their fault.

IN every insurance policy the big print giveth and the small print taketh away.

MY carma ran over your dogma.

WHEN it comes to used cars it's hard to drive a bargain.

USED cars are alright, as far as they go.

WHY do you have to spend $5 to park your car to avoid a $50 fine while spending 50 cents on a cup of coffee?

THE main reason people drive more than they once did is because it is cheaper to drive than park.

THE driver is safer when the roads are dry, and the roads are safer when the driver is dry.

DO you remember the good old days when the only trouble with parking was to get the girl to agree?

"WOULD you like to get in the back seat?" he asked when he parked the car.
   "Can't I stay in the front seat with you?" she replied.

YOUNG people should be careful when parking because accidents cause people.

ON the road there is no fool like an oiled fool.

FAMOUS last words: Well, if he won't dip his lights I won't dip mine.

IT'S getting to the point where a person killed in a car accident is considered to have died a natural death.

Travel

I'VE just returned from a pleasure trip. I've just driven the wife to the airport.

TRAVEL advice: Don't put all your bags in one exit.

IF you see an unattended bag, go up and talk to her.

REMEMBER, it is easier to find a travelling companion than to get rid of one.

AT the airport Trevor the traveller abused the luggage handler. His case comes up next week.

HE told the travel agent: "I want a round world ticket."
   She said, "One way, or return?"

MY uncle is a mental traveller. His mind wanders.

ONE hundred years ago they said flying was impossible.
Today, most of us agree.

HOW often do jumbo jets crash?
Just the once.

IT was one of those cheap flights. Instead of an inflight movie the pilot flew low over the drive-in theatres.

"CONTROL tower to Air Lingus, what's your height and position?"
"Captain Murphy to control. I'm foive-feet two and I'm sitting up the front."

I MET my wife at a travel agency. She was looking for a holiday and I was the last resort.

A RESORT is where the locals live off your holiday until next summer.

I GOT one of those bargain packages, seven days and two nights.

THE wife went to a travel agent and asked where she could go for $50. He told her.

SHE was on the phone from the Gold Coast. "The holiday is wonderful darling, I feel like a new woman."
"So do I. Stay there another week."

SOME people travel for a change and a rest only to find the hotel takes the change and the taxi takes the rest.

THE Jewish travel agent sold a ticket for the new Hovercraft ferry which would cross the channel at full speed. "But for you, half-speed," he said.

Graffiti

NO doubt about it, brevity is the soul of wit and ever since man could write he has written on walls in short, sharp slogans that were "politically incorrect" until many were adopted by the general populace.
The walls of our cities have long been the only form of published expression available to crusaders of causes that have eventually changed society.
  As Paul Simon wrote:
  "The words of the prophet
  Are written on the subway halls,
  And tenement walls."

FREE Collective Bargaining. He's innocent.

JUST because you're not paranoid doesn't mean they are not out to get you.

IGNORE This Sign.

SUICIDE is the most sincere form of self-criticism.

GET Maggier Thatcher before she gets ...ugh...ugh!

TIME flies like bullets, fruit flies like bananas.

OWING to lack of interest tomorrow has been cancelled.

BUT for Venetian blinds it would be curtains for us all.

Y-FRONTS prevent fall out.

CALLING all animal lovers. We wish to inform you that your habits are illegal.

NOT enough is being done for the Apathetic.

WHAT made Elizabeth Arden? When Max Factor.

SEX is alright, but it's not the real thing.

ELVIS Lives! (And they've buried the poor bugger).

ELVIS rocks in his box.

YESTERDAY I couldn't spell engineer.
   Today I are one.

I NEVER used to be able to finish anything, but now I ...

YORICK is a numb skull.

TURK, Jew or Atheist
   May enter here,
   But not a Papist!

... to which a reply was later chalked:
Who wrote this wrote it well
For the same is written
On the Gates of Hell.

WHY do people write, "Fuck the Pope" on walls?
  Because there is usually very little room, or time, to
write: "Fuck the Moderator of the General Assembly
of the Church of Scotland."

THE country is stuffed through apathy!
  (What's Apathy?)
  (I don't know and I don't care).

GOD Lives!
  (So does Doubting Thomas).

JESUS Saves!
  (Moses invests).
  (But only Buddha pays dividends).

JESUS Saves!
  (But the Mongol hordes).

JESUS Saves!
  (He couldn't on my salary).

JESUS Saves!
  (Darwin survives).

JESUS Lives!
  (Does this mean no Easter holidays?)

THE meek shall inherit the earth
  (They're not game to refuse it).

THE meek shall inherit the earth
  (If that's okay by the rest of you?)

LEGALISE Mental Telepathy.
  (I knew you were going to say that).

GRAFFITI should be obscene and not heard.

GRAFFITI was Mussolini's Secretary for Defence.

AYATOLLAH Khomeini is a Shiite.

DEATH is Life's answer to the question Why?

DEATH is the price of Evolution.

REINCARNATION is a pleasant surprise.

THE cleaner's work has been in vain
  The phantom sprayer has struck again!

SIGN on hotel wall:
  Count your change. Some of our staff are in business for themselves.

ALL the big women die young.
  That's why we are left with little old ladies.

IF it has to be a matter of Reds under the bed, please send me Natasha.

ORAL sex is a matter of taste.

ANARCHISTS unite!

EUNUCHS unite! You have nothing to lose.

YOU can tell the sex of a chromosome by taking down its genes.

ROSE'S are red, Violet's are blue and Jean isn't wearing any.

LITTLE Red Riding Hood is a Russian contraceptive.

OEDIPUS was the first man to plug the generation gap.

SADO-MASOCHISM means not having to say you are sorry.

IF you feel strongly about graffiti, sign a partition.

LIFE is a sexually transmitted disease.

I CHOKED Linda Lovelace.

UNTIL I discovered women I thought love was a pain in the arse.

LOWER the age of puberty.

WAKE up to insomnia.

I AM an abject failure:
    Legalise abortion!

SUPPORT fee enterprise:
    Legalise prostitution!

STAMP out philately!

STAMP out quicksand!

REPEAL the law of gravity.

REPEAL the banana.

DEPRESSIVE neurosis is nothing to laugh about.

REALITY is for people who can't cope with drugs.

BE placid with acid.

GRASS is nature's way of saying: "High."

HELP a nun kick the habit!

HIRE the morally handicapped.

SILENCE those who oppose freedom of speech.

WE are the people our parents warned us about.

LIFE is a hereditary disease. And terminal.

THOSE who think they know it all upset those of us
who do!

I'D give my right arm to be ambidextrous.

WHAT has posterity ever done for me?

NOSTALGIA isn't what it used to be.
    It's a thing of the past.

LARGE cats can be dangerous,
   but a little pussy never hurt anyone.

TO go together is blessed,
   to come together is divine.

I AM virgin on the edge of intercourse.

IT'S all very graffitifying.

12
The Family,
Relatively Speaking

Family

YOU can't choose your ancestors, but that's fair enough for they probably wouldn't have chosen you. However, the beauty of rearing a large family is the hope that at least one of them may not turn out like the others.

SUCCESS is relative. The more success the more relatives.

LET'S not be hard on our relatives. After all, they had no say in the matter either.

OEDIPUS was the first man to plug the generation gap.

ANY one of your friends can become an enemy, given time, but a relative is one from the start.

A CLOSE relative may be a skinflint, yet he may the skinflint you love to touch.

MY brother is in medical science.
    He's not studying anything. They are studying him.

MY brother hates daylight saving.

He gets his morning erection on the train.

EVERY family should have at least three children. Then if one is a genius the other two can support him.

FREE speech is practised by teenagers who reverse the charges.

SHE took after the mother, who took after the father, who took after the maid.

MONTY can trace his family tree back to when it was his ancestors' address.

A GREAT many prominent family trees were started by grafting.

HEREDITY runs in our family.

ATHLETES run in the family.

NOSES run in ours.

WHAT'S an orgasm, Mum?"

"Don't know. Ask your father."

"MUM, Dad's going out again!"

"Well pour some more petrol on him."

THE cheapest way of tracing your family tree is to nominate for politics.

THERE were 15 of us in our family. I didn't know what it was like to sleep alone until I got married.

THE doctor asked if there was any insanity in the family. "Yes," said Mum. "My husband thinks he's the boss."

WE treated the guest like one of the family. So he went home.

THERE is no place like home, which is why I go out every night.

GIVE me a home, where the buffalo roam, and I'll show you a house full of bullshit.

SOME adults blame juvenile delinquency on everything but heredity.

ONE of the great mysteries of family life is where the parents learnt about all the things they tell their children not to do.

THE walls of our unit were so thin that once I asked my wife a question and got three different answers.

Kids

KIDS are the ultimate contraceptive.

THEY say children brighten the home. That's because they never turn the bloody lights off.

A CHILD is a creature that stands halfway between an adult and the television set.

MEMBERS of the younger generation are all alike in many disrespects.

CHILDREN should be seen and not had.

CHILDREN, what a comfort in old age. And how soon they bring it on.

ONE child is not enough, but two are far too many.

IN the old days people considered children as necessities and cars as luxuries; now they're reversed.

BLESSED are the young for they shall inherit the national debt.

HEREDITY is something people believe in if they have a bright child.

THE conceited father said it was clear that their genius infant son had inherited his intelligence from him.
    "Must have," said his wife, "I've still got mine."

IF your parents didn't have any children, chances are you won't either.

KIDS never put off till tomorrow what will keep them from going to bed tonight.

THE hardest thing in the world is to raise a child, especially in the morning.

DO your children a favour. Don't have any.

I'VE got three kids. One of each.

I ALWAYS wanted to spend more time with my kids. Then one day I did.

SANTA Claus has no kids. He only comes once a year, and then it's down a chimney.

JUST when the children get old enough so that you can stand them, they can't stand you.

ADOLESCENCE is that stage between infancy and adultery.

THE note from the teacher read: "Your son's writing is so bad we can't tell if he can spell or not."

THE easiest way to teach children the value of money is to borrow some from them.

PARENTS spend the first three years of a child's life trying to get it to talk, and the next 16 years trying to get it to shut up.

PRIDE is something you feel when your kids run a garage sale and raise a few hundred dollars. Panic is when you go to get your car and find it gone.

SMALL boy watching his mum do the washing: "Mum, where did you work before you got this job here with us?"

"MUMMY, you know the vase you were always worried I would break? Well your worries are over."

Teenagers

TODAY'S teenagers are alike in many disrespects.

TEENAGE girls are between pigtails and cocktails.

TEENAGE boys complain that there is nothing to do, then stay out all night doing it.

TEENAGERS think curbing their emotions means parking by the roadside.

THE adolescent's life from 12 to 18 can add 20 years to a parent's life.

WISE parents should pin a notice on a teenager's door: "Check-out time is 18."

SHE is at the awkward age. She has stopped asking where she came from and refuses to say where she is going.

HE is going through an awkward age. He is changing from a hooligan to a layabout.

Mothers-in-Law

FEW mistakes can be made by a mother-in-law willing to babysit.

BEHIND every successful man there stands a surprised mother-in-law.

MY mother-in-law broke up our marriage.
   My wife found me in bed with her.

THE ransom note read: "We have captured your mother-in-law. If you don't pay the ransom we will send her back."

MY mother-in-law thinks I am effiminate.
   Compared to her I probably am.

ACTUALLY, she was thrown out of the Mafia, for cruelty.

NOW she is in show business. She is just back from a successful season at Loch Ness.

THE local Peeping Tom knocked on the door the other night and asked if the mother-in-law would mind closing her bedroom curtains.

I NEVER forget a face. But in my mother-in-law's case, I am willing to make an exception.

THE last time she came to see us it was pouring with rain. I opened the door and there she was. I said: "Don't stand there in the pouring rain, go home."

FOR 20 years my mother-in-law and I were happy.
   Then we met.

THE penalty for bigamy is two mothers-in-law.

I KEEP telling my wife that I like her mother-in-law a lot better than I like mine.

WHEN I told my mother-in-law that our house was her house, she sold it.

THEY'RE strange. One day I'm not good enough for her daughter, the next I've fathered the brightest grandchild on earth.

MARRIAGE Anonymous is a club for bachelors. If any member is tempted to wed they send over a mother-in-law in a dressing gown and hair curlers.

Neighbours

EVER since we put the "Neighbourhood Watch" sign on our gate every bastard comes in and wants to know the time.

IT'S been tough keeping up with the Joneses.
   Especially since Tom moved next door.

DON'T keep trying to keep up with the Joneses. Drag them down to your level.

MANY a successful man owes it to the Joneses.

WE'VE made a deal with the neighbours. We'll stop trying to keep up with them if they'll stop trying to keep up with us.

HE knocked on the door and said: "I'm looking for the people who live here."
   "Well you've come to the right place."

Friends

A FRIEND is someone who goes around saying nice things about you behind your back.

A FRIEND in need is a pest indeed.

A FRIEND in need is a frequent occurrence.

BE nice to your friends. If it wasn't for them you'd be a total stranger.

A FRIEND is a person who dislikes the same people you do.

IF you help a friend in trouble he is bound to remember you, especially next time he is in trouble.

THE redeeming point about enemies is that they never come around pestering you and borrowing things.

THE surest way to destroy your enemies is to make them your friends.

ALWAYS label the Christmas presents you receive from your friends. That way you won't give them to the wrong people next year.

IT'S what your guests say as they swing out of your driveway that counts.

WHEN you know nothing but good about a person, it is more fun to talk about somebody else.

Ourselves

I HAVE no self confidence. If a woman says "yes" to me I advise her to think it over.

I ALWAYS thought I was a failure until they taught me to be positive. Now I'm positive I'm a failure.

IF my father hadn't been so shy and reserved I would be five years older than I am.

I AM a success in one way. I started out with nothing and still have most of it.

MY ambition is to marry a rich girl who is too proud to let her husband work.

HALF the lies they tell about me are not true.

IT'S strange how we expect to get more out of a camera than we put in.

WE complain about the ridiculous photo in our passport without realising it looks exactly as our friends see us.

IF other people are going to talk, then conversation becomes impossible.

WHEN I was a kid I was pretty stupid. I didn't realise I was 10 until I was 13.

I WAS the kind of kid my parents told me not to play with.

YOU know you're insecure when you play hide and seek at a party and nobody comes to find you.

IT is very embarrassing to be mistaken at the top of our voice.

IF you are trying to kill time always make sure it is your own.

YOU can fool all the people some of the time, but you can fool yourself all the time.

IF you keep your mouth shut you can fool a lot of people.

THE most inconsiderate person is the one who wants me to listen when I want to talk.

IF you wish to be a good sport you must let people teach you a lot of things you already know.

WE keep on making history because we don't learn from it.

WE learn nothing from history, except that we learn nothing from history.

TO forget wrong is the best revenge. And the only people worth getting even with are those who helped you.

TOLERANCE is that uncomfortable feeling that the other bloke may be right after all.

I DON'T mind suffering in silence, provided every-body knows I'm doing it.

Dogs

I FINALLY managed to teach my dog to beg. Last night he came home with $15.

MY dog is so obedient. I only have to say the word "attack" and he has one.

MY dog's so obedient,
   He does as he's bid,
   The sign said "Wet Paint,"
   And that's what he did.

I'VE got a useless Dobermann pinscher. All it does is pinch Dobermanns.

I BOUGHT a wild pitbull terrier, but in no time I had it eating out of my leg.

I'VE got a miniature poodle. The minute I turn my back he does a poodle.

I'VE got a dog called Mechanic. When you kick him in the nuts he makes a bolt for the door.

I'VE got a dog called Carpenter. He's always doing little jobs around the house.

MY dog has such a pedigree that, if he could talk, he wouldn't speak to either of us.

THERE'S a new brand of pet food called "Woof!"
It's the brand dogs ask for by name.

FRED put some Spot remover on his dog, now he can't find it.

MERV took his dog to the flea circus and the mutt stole the show.

"I THINK your dog likes me, Gladys, he hasn't taken his eyes off me all night."
"That's because you're eating off his plate."

A MAN who came home and found his wife in bed with his best friend shot the wife, but decided to give the dog another chance.

FIDO is not much of a poker player. Every time he gets a good hand he wags his tail.

MY dog took first prize at a cat show. He took the cat.

THE Buddhist knocked on the vicar's door and said: "My carma just ran over your dogma."

WE'VE got a fine watch dog. So far he was watched somebody steal our car, watched the garage burn down and watched a bloke pinch the lawn mower.

TWO dogs met on the street. "What's your name?" said one.
"I'm not sure. I think it's Down Boy."

WHY do dogs lick their balls?
Because they can.

Birthdays

I WOULD have been two years older if my father hadn't been so shy and retiring.

MY wife gave me a smoking jacket for my birthday. It took me an hour to put it out.

IF it is really the thought that counts very few of us would ever get presents.

THE biggest surprise you can give your wife on her birthday is to remember it.

THE man who forgets his wife's birthday will get something to remember it by.

I NEVER forget my wife's birthday. It is always the day after she reminds me of it.

HUSBAND'S defence: "How am I expected to remember your birthday when you never look a day older?"

A DIPLOMAT is the man who sends 25 roses to a woman on her 31st birthday.

SHE said she was looking forward to her 29th birthday, but we're certain she's looking in the wrong direction.

SHE'S just turned 32, but the way she's turned it makes her 23.

HERE'S to you. No matter how old you are you certainly don't look it.

WHEN a man has a birthday he takes a day off. When a woman has a birthday she takes a year off.

SHE was born in the year of Our Lord only knows.

"I DON'T think I look 35, do you?" she asked her husband.
   "No, I don't," he said, "but you used to."

Names

THE study of names is fascinating. For example did you know that the name Howard means "clever", and that John means "not-very"?

DARLING is the wife's maiden name.

RUTH is stranger than fiction.

MY brother was called Seven-and-a-quarter. They picked his name out of a hat.

WE have a young brother called Onyx. Why?
   Because he was onyxpected.

WE have another called Isaiah. Why?
   Because one eye's 'igher than the other.

WE had a third who was named after my father.
   We called him Dad.

I WAS fortunate to be named George.
   Because that's what everybody calls me.

A PSEUDONYM is a nym that is not your real nym.

MONTY has just changed his name by deed poll to
CMH-869 so that he could have personalised number
plates.

I ONCE had a dog called Mechanic. Give him a kick
in the nuts and he'd make a bolt for the door.

I HAD another pup called Carpenter. He used to do
little jobs around the house.

I WAS born on the first of the month so they named
me Bill.

"WHAT'S the name of your parents?"
   "Mum and Dad."

"ARE you chewing gum?"
   "No. I'm Harry McGillicardy."

SHE said she loved men who were frank.
   He said he was sorry his name was Algernon.

ASKED what was the new baby's name Paddy replied,
"Don't know. We can't understand a damned word he
says."

"HEY, Fred. What's Billie's other name?"
   "Billie who?"

"DO you know my wife, May?"

"No, I didn't. Thanks for the tip."

PEOPLE with hyphenated names are unlikely to have a sense of humour.

A WOMAN will always be second fiddle to a bloke who gives a nickname to his dick.

NEVER go out with anyone who answers when you call them dick-head.

IF your surname is Pipe don't call the baby Dwayne.

IF your surname is Long, don't call the baby Miles.

IN the doctor's waiting room one bloke said he was aching from arthritis, the other replied that he was Murphy from Dublin and a third said he was little stiff from Badminton.

13
Growing Old Disgracefully

Middle age

MIDDLE age is when you have a choice of two temptations and you take the one that will still get you home early.

MIDDLE age is when you are sitting at home on Saturday night, the phone rings and you hope it isn't for you.

MIDDLE age is when you would like to stand up and give your seat to the lady, but can't.

Old codgers

THE best thing to save for old age, is yourself.

IF I knew how old I was going to get I would have taken more care of myself.

DO not resist growing old. Many are denied the privilege.

AS the old codger said: "If they had electric blankets and sliced bread in my day I would have never got married."

ANYONE who stops learning is old; whether it happens at twenty or eighty.

AGE is a matter of attitude. I am retreaded, not retired.

YOU are getting old when you don't care where your wife goes, just so long as you don't have to go along too.

YOU know you're old when your back goes out more than you do.

YOU know you are old when you look at the menu instead of the waitress.

YOU know you're old when you sit in a rocking chair and can't make it go.

You know you're old when your pacemaker activates the garage door when a pretty girl goes by.

YOU know you're old when you have a dicky heart, instead of the other way round.

YOU know you are getting old when people refer to you as "young-looking" instead of young.

YOU know you are getting old when you bend down to tie your shoe laces and try to think if there is anything else needs doing while you're down there.

THEY told him he was amazing for his age.
    "Nothing amazing about it," he said. "All I've done is grow old and taken longer than most people to do it."

BY the time you reach 75 years of age you've learnt everything. All you have to do is to try and remember it.

BY the time a man can afford to lose a golf ball, he can't hit that far.

POP remembers the times when beer was threepence a loaf.

HE can remember when the village square was a place, not a person.

HE can remember when the wonder drugs were mustard plaster and castor oil.

HE remembers the day he gave up booze and sex at the same time. "Gawd. That was the worst half-hour I've ever spent!"

THE secret of longevity is deep breathing, as long as you can keep it up for eighty years.

YOU can live much longer if you give up everything that makes you want to live longer.

AFTER you lose your membership in it, the younger generation looks pretty bad.

THE old rake said he was getting so old he couldn't take yes for an answer. And he didn't think he would lust much longer.

WHEN a woman says no, he's grateful.

MY Uncle Fred lived to 100 and owed it all to mushrooms. He never ate any.

THE dapper old gent asked the barber if he had anything for grey hair.
"Only the deepest respect," he said.

ON his 80th birthday his friends hired a hooker who said: "Hi, pops, I'm here for supersex!"
"Good," he said, "Then I'll have the soup."

"HAVE you lived all your life in this village?"
  "Not yet."

"TO what do you attribute your long life?"
  "To being born so long ago."

AUNT Maud dreamt she was married.
  But when she woke up she found there was nothing in it.

A GERIATRIC is a German cricketer who captures three successive wickets.

Grannies

NO cowboy was faster on the draw than a grandmother producing baby photos from her purse.

WE finally figured out how to stop Granny biting her nails. We made her keep her boots on.

WHAT'S got 75 balls and screws old grannies?
  Bingo.

WHEN Grandpa went to join the Returned Soldiers' League they asked him if he had a war record: "Bloody oath. I've got Vera Lynn singing the White Cliffs of Dover."

Age from a woman's perspective

A YOUTHFUL figure is what you get when you ask a woman her age.

THE age of a woman is like the speedo on a car.

You know it's been set back but you don't know how far.

"HOW old would a person be who was born in 1930?" asked the teacher.

"Man or woman?" replied the smart pupil.

"I DON'T look 30 do I?"

"No, but you did when you were."

"I DON'T know how old she is, but she certainly doesn't look it."

SHE says she is is close to 30, but she won't say from which side.

SOME of the happiest years of a woman's life are when she is 29.

14
Affairs of the Heart

From courtship, to proposals, engagements, the odd pre-marital bonk, marriage and divorce.

Openers, or cheeky chat-ups

IT was Mae West who dropped the famous line: "Is that a gun in your pocket, or are you just glad to see me." Here's a few more "sin openers" that may assist those interested in a cheeky chat-ups.

I WAS having alphabet soup the other day and your name came up.

I DON'T believe we've met. I'm Mr Right.

WHAT about a date? No obligations. If we are not compatible then you can put your clothes on and go home.

I AM a lecturer in social psychology. Do you mind if I bore the pants off you?

"EXCUSE me, I'm a stranger here. Can you direct me to your home?"

"YOU'RE just my type. You're a girl!"

"WOULD you like to come up to my room and look at the ceiling for awhile?"

"EXCUSE me, I don't normally talk to strangers but I'm on my way to confession and I'm short on material".

WOULD you come up to my flat and help me write my will?

IMPROVE your image and be seen with me.

TELL me about yourself, your dreams, your ambitions, your phone number.

PARDON me, I'm writing a phone book. Can I have your number?

"EXCUSE me, can I have your number?"
     "It's in the book."
     "Oh. And what is your name?"
     "That's in the book too."

THERE is a secret password which always breaks the ice with dumb blondes. It's "Hello."

HI Babe, like to sit on my wallet?

And the woman's approach:

"YOU look like my third husband."
     "How many have you had?"
     "Two."

SORRY, I can't go out Saturday night, I'm expecting a headache.

"WHERE have I been all your life? Well for the first half I wasn't born."

Bachelors

HE who lives without quarrelling is a bachelor.

A BACHELOR is a man who is footloose and fiancée-free.

A BACHELOR is a man who never chases a woman he can't outrun.

HE'S a bachelor by choice, mainly by choice of the women he's been out with.

A BACHELOR is a man who has cheated some poor woman out of a divorce settlement.

A BACHELOR is a man whose marriage vow is never to take one.

A BACHELOR is a man who can cook, wash and darn his own socks in case he gets married one day.

A BACHELOR is a fellow who believes he is entitled to life, liberty and the happiness of pursuit.

HIS ambition is to be the last man on earth, so he can find out if all those women were telling the truth.

Spinsters

A spinster is a girl who's phone doesn't ring, even when she's in the bath.

THE only person who has asked her to get married is her mother.

Courting

HE approached her father and with hand on his heart said: "Sir, the bright sunshine of your daughter's smile has blown away the dark clouds on my life's horizon ..." The father stopped him and said: "Is this a proposal or a weather forecast." That was the old style. These one-liners cover today's affairs of the heart from courting to divorce.

MANY a young suitor browses through the family album failing to heed the warnings.

MANY a man works hard to keep the wolf from the door. Then his daughter grows up and brings one right into the house.

YOU can always attract the girl's favourable attention by getting her parents to dislike you.

COURTSHIP is the time during which the girl decides whether or not she can do any better.

IF all men are alike, why do women find it so hard to pick one?

SOME girls keep their love letters, others let their love letters keep them.

BEING seduced is a matter of perfect timing.
 The woman has to give in, just before the man gives up.

HE said he had come to ask for his daughter's hand.
 "Okay, take the one that always in my pocket."

THERE is nothing so expensive than a woman who is free for the evening.

IT was only weeks after he got engaged to the circus contortionist that she broke it off.

SOME joyrides extend from here to maternity.

'TIS love that makes the world go round, with that worried expression.

"WILL you respect me in the morning?"
 "Of course, especially if you're good at it."

"DON'T the stars look lovely tonight?"
 "Can't tell," he replied, "I'm in no position to say."

"DON'T you know what good clean fun is?"
 "No. What good is it?"

"AM I the first man to make love to you?"
 "Of course you are," she replied, "Why do all men ask the same stupid question?"

"OH, don't do that," she said, "or I'll go to pieces."

"Go ahead," he replied, "I've got the piece I want.

SHE finally got fed up with her boyfriend's fumbling advances and decided to put him in her place.

ALL is fair in love and the war which follows.

"DO you like big weddings or little ones?"

"Without big weddings you shouldn't have little ones."

"SIR, I want your daughter for my wife."

"Well, I'm not swapping until I've seen your wife."

IF a bloke looks a girl right in the eye he may be missing other things she hoped he would notice.

IF they became engaged she wanted to know if she would get a ring.

"Certainly, what's your number?"

FRED'S been turned down so many times he is like the hot page in a naughty novel.

THEIR courtship was fast and furious. She was fast and he was furious.

SOME women can't be trusted too far.

And some men can't be trusted too near.

ANY girl that spends hours spooning obviously isn't the type that's easily stirred.

HE snuggled up to her and said: "I'm yours for the asking."

She snuggled back and said: "I'm asking fifty bucks!"

"I CAN'T marry you Claude," she said. "I prefer a man who is making things, like that Mr Finklestein who makes half a million a year."

WEDDING proposals are different these days. The boy doesn't say "Will you marry me." He says: "You're gonna have a what?"

IT takes a lot of experience for a girl to kiss like a beginner.

WHEN Adam and Eve were courting he said: "Wow, where on earth did you learn to kiss like that?"

A WOMAN doesn't believe a man who says he is unworthy of her until they are married.

"I HEAR you are engaged. Who's the lucky woman?"

"Her mother."

SHE said to the vicar: "Do you believe in sex before marriage?"

"So long as you don't block the aisle," he replied.

AFTER a passionate session he said: "Darling, was I the first?"

"Why do men always ask that question?" she said.

DON'T marry anyone until you've seen them drunk.

ON my wedding night I stood in front of my bride in my birthday suit. She said it needed ironing.

FROM courting to marriage is from dating to intimi-dating.

MY lady be wary of Cupid,
    And list to the words of this verse,
    To let a fool kiss you is stupid,
    To let a kiss fool you is worse.

TRY not to snore during foreplay.

THREE little words, "I love you," can inflate the ego.
    Three little words, "Is it in," can deflate the ego.

15
The Splice of Life

Weddings

GIRLS usually marry men who remind them of their fathers, which is why most of their mothers cry.

A FRIENDSHIP which began when they were at high school ended in marriage yesterday.

THE father is the bloke who spends thousands of dollars on the wedding then reads in the paper that he gave the bride away.

WHEN the minister said "for better or for worse," he meant the groom couldn't do better and the bride couldn't do worse.

MARRIAGE is the price men pay for sex, and sex is the price women pay for marriage.

A WEDDING is oceans of emotions surrounded by expanses of expenses.

HE took her for better or for worse. She took him for everything.

A BRIDE'S attitude to her groom can be summed up in three words: "Aisle. Altar. Hymn."

A SHOTGUN wedding is a case of wife or death.

THERE is so much permissiveness in the world today that the only way to stop having sex is to get married.

AT the altar he thinks: "Wow! Free sex from now on."
  She thinks: "Wow! No more sex from now on."

HAPPY is the bride that the sun of a tycoon takes a shine to today.

SHE had turned 30 and had been difficult to unload. When her father finally gave her away at the altar he demanded a receipt.

THE bride insisted the wedding should be perfect. "We mustn't overlook the most insignificant detail."
  "Don't worry," said her mother, "he'll show up."

THE relative from out of town arrived late. "Who gave the bride away?" he asked.
  "Any one of us could, but we all agreed to keep our mouths shut."

AFTER a few champagnes the tipsy young bride stood up to thank the guests for the presents. "... and I'd like to thank my parents-in-law for giving me such a perky copulator."

EVEN these days there are a few four-letter words which can still shock most brides, like cook, wash, dust and iron.

A WISE bride is one who makes her husband feel as if he is master of the house, when in reality he is only chairman of the entertainment committee.

A BRIDE is a woman who puts her foot down as soon as she is carried over the threshold.

A BRIDEGROOM is a bloke who is amazed at the outcome of what he thought was a little flirtation.

THE bride wept, the bridesmaids wept, even the wedding cake was in tiers.

AS the groom said: "Here today, gone home to Momma."

MURPHY and his bride sat up all night waiting for their sexual relations to arrive.

SHE married a sailor because she wanted to have children and rear admirals.

I WILL never forget my wedding. God knows I've tried.

A WEDDING is a funeral where you smell your own flowers.

A WEDDING ring is a one man band.

THERE was a little man
   And he had a little gun
   And his bullets were made of lead
   He stood close by
   With a fatherly eye
   While me and my girl were wed.

Wedding speeches

LADIES and gentlemen, what can I say about the groom that hasn't already been said in court.

IN many ways (the groom) has been like a son to me; insolent, ungrateful, disrespectful.

LADIES, and gentlemen, I will only speak for a few minutes because of my throat. If I go on too long my wife has threatened to cut it.

LADIES, and gentlemen, I had a feeling it was going to be difficult to follow a speech by John. I was right, I couldn't follow a bloody word of it.

LADIES, and gentlemen. We all know a lot about John, but in the interests of harmony and in order not to embarrass the bride I intend to dwell only on the pleasant side of his character. Thank you very much (and go to sit down).

LADIES, and gentlemen. The Ladies is over there (*point*) and the Gents is over there (*point*).

THE groom will be getting up to speak in a moment or two and I can tell you he has some very interesting material, starting with his suit.

I ASKED my wife if she remembered our wedding night. She said it was 25 years ago and there was no need to apologise now.

AFTER we had been married a month I said to her, "You don't mind if I point out a few of your faults?"

She said, "Not at all. It's those little faults that stopped me getting a better husband."

Response from bridegrooms:

I WOULD like to thank my new father for those kind words. It's remarkable what some people will say when not under oath.

WHEN I asked him if I could marry his daughter he said: "Just leave your name and phone number. If nothing better comes up we'll give you a bell."

OUR thanks must go to our parents. Without them none of this would be possible.

THIS is the happiest day of my life, and I really must thank my bride for pointing this out.

I REALLY couldn't ask for a better woman. If I did she'd kill me.

I WOULD like to thank the bridesmaids. They performed their role perfectly and I will certainly re-hire them if I ever get married again.

And to get on side with the mother-in-law:

THEY say a girl grows to be like her mother. Well, I can only hope it is true.

Telegrams

TO the groom:

"Congratulations Gerald. It was better to have loved and lost than never to have loved at all. Signed, Mary, Terese, Wendy, Karen, Julie, Barbara, Estelle and Agatha."

IT was better to have loved a short girl than never to have loved a tall.

TO the bride:

"Congratulations from your loving mother. Twenty-two years ago I sent you to bed with a dummy. Tonight history repeats itself."

Wedding toasts: (See Toasts for all occasions P223)

TO the happy couple. May they lie, cheat and steal.
    May they lie in each other's arms,
    May they cheat Father Time,
    And may they often steal away to renew their love and affection.

A TOAST to love and laughter, and happiness ever after.

HERE'S to the husband, here's to the wife,
    May they be lovers for the rest of their life.

DOWN the hatch, to a striking match.

HERE'S to the newly-weds. May we all be invited to their Golden Wedding Anniversary.

HERE'S to your wedding, and many of them.

MAY all your ups and downs be in bed.

Groom's toast:

HERE'S to my mother-in-law's daughter,
   Here's to my father-in-law's son,
   And here's to the vows we've just taken,
   And the life that we've just begun.

HERE'S to the happiest days of my life,
   Spent in the arms of another man's wife,
   My mother's.

HERE'S to the groom with bride so fair,
   And here's to the bride with groom so rare.

HERE'S to our sweethearts and our wives,
   May our sweethearts soon become our wives,
   And our wives still remain our sweethearts.

Honeymoons

THE honeymoon is over when he phones to say he will be late, but she has already left a note to say dinner is in the oven.

HE knew the honeymoon was over when everything she said, and cooked, disagreed with him.

THE current trend is towards shorter honeymoons, but usually more of them.

THE boss asked the intended groom how much leave he wanted for his honeymoon. "How long do you think?"

"I don't know," said the boss, "I haven't seen the bride."

16
Toasts for all Occasions

ONE of society's cherished traditions is the raised glass and the sincere expression of goodwill that is expressed in the toast. It is a major purpose of this book to provide a wide range of options.Toasts can relay any message of emotion, from love, sentimental, cynicism, comical or downright bawdy. First, a word on toastmasters:

THE toastmaster rises between the meal and the speaker and tries to pretend that the latter won't be as unpalatable as the former.

TO be a master of the toast you need to know when to pop up and when to pop down.

"FORNICATION," roared the MC, "fornication like this we need champagne for the toast..."

ABSENT friends!

LONG life to you, and may you die in your own bed.

EAT, drink and be merry for tomorrow we diet.

MAY wayward monks have a double Lent.

MAY Lady Fortune smile on you all for the rest of your life, and may you never know her daughter (Mis Fortune).

MAY every man become what he thinks himself to be.

MAY our (*guest*) live for a hundred years, and may we all be there to count them.

MAY you live as long as you want, and may you never want as long as you live.

MAY the undertakers never overtake us.

HERE'S champagne to our true friends, and pain to our sham friends.

HERE'S to the kisses you've snatched,
    and vice versa.

HERE'S to the girl who lives on the hill
    She won't be in it, but her sister will
    Here's to her sister, then.

HERE'S to your genitalia
    May it never land you in jailiya

HERE'S to the friend who knows you well, and likes you just the same.

HERE'S to eternity. May we spend it in as good company as this night finds us.

HERE'S to women, the only beloved autocrats who govern without law and decide without appeal.

HERE'S to a full belly, a heavy purse and a light heart.

HERE'S that we may live to eat,
   the hen that scratches on our grave.

HERE'S to our health. May it remain with us long after we're dead.

HERE'S to our hostess, considerate and sweet,
   Her wit is endless, but when do we eat?

HERE'S to Hell, and may the stay there,
   Be as much fun as on the way there.

HERE'S to a clear conscience,
   And a poor memory.

IF you are big enough, your troubles will always be smaller than you are.

WE can never do a kindness to our friends too soon, because we never know how soon it may be too late.

HERE'S to long corns and short shoes to our enemies.

MAY the fleas of a thousand camels infest the underpants of our enemies.

MAY your chooks turn into emus and kick down your dunny door.

MAY we all get to heaven half an hour before the devil knows we're dead.

MAY the skin of your bum never cover a drum.

MAY you live a hundred years, and another month to repent.

MAY we never put our finger in another man's pie.

MAY you never have to eat your hat.

MAY the frost never afflict your spuds.

MAY the Blue Bird of Happiness crap down your chimney.

MAY we all be alive this time, twelve months.

MAY you slide down the bannister of life, with nary a splinter.

MAY your luck be like the capital of Ireland, always Dublin!

HERE'S to the bloke down the lane
    He courted a girl, all in vain
    She swore when he kissed her
    So he slept with her sister
    Again and again and again.

HERE'S to a long life and a merry one,
    A quick death, and a painless one,
    A pretty woman, and a loving one,
    A cold bottle, and another one.

TO our wives and sweethearts. May they never meet.

HERE'S to your eyes, and mine
    Here's to your lips, and mine
    The former have met
    The latter not yet
    So here's to that moment, sublime.

HERE'S to Miss Prim
    For her life held no terrors
    Born a virgin, died a virgin
    No hits, no runs, no errors.

LONG live Centenarians.

HERE'S to us
    May we live a long life
    And here's mud in your eye
    While I wink at your wife.

To Love:

LET'S drink to love. Which is nothing,
    unless it's divided by two.

MAY love draw the curtain,
    And friendship the cork.

I HAVE know many, liked a few,
    Loved but one, so here's to you.
    MAY you live as long as you want to
    And want to, as long as you live.

MAY we kiss who we please
    And please who we kiss.

HERE'S to love that begins with a fever and ends with a yawn.

HERE'S to love and unity,
   Dark corners and opportunity.

HERE'S to the land we love, and the love we land.

COME in the evening, come in the morning,
   Come when you are looked for, or come without warning.

SAY it with flowers,
   Say it with sweets,
   Say it with kisses,
   Say it with eats,
   Say it with jewellery,
   Say it with drink,
   But be bloody careful,
   Not to say it with ink.

To yourself:
HERE'S to you, and here's to me.
   But as you're not here, then it's two for me.

HERE'S to you, and here's to me,
   And may we never disagree.
   But if we do, to Hell with you,
   ...and here's to me.

HERE'S to me. I've finally found what's unbelievable,
   A sex-mad maid who's inconceivable.

OVER my teeth around my gums,
    Look out belly, here it comes.

Christening toast:

A NEW life begun, like father, like son.
    or
LIKE one, like the other, like mother like daughter.

Anniversary toast:

HERE'S to you both, a beautiful pair,
    On the birthday of your love affair.

Women's toasts:

TO the men I've loved,
    To the men I've kissed,
    My heartfelt apologies,
    To the men I've missed.

HERE'S to the night I met you.
    If I hadn't met you, I wouldn't have let you.
    Now that I've let you, I'm glad that I met you.
    And I'll let you again, I will bet you.

IF I'm asleep when you want me. Wake me.
    And if I don't want to. Make me.

IF I am sleeping
    and you want to, wake me,
    don't shake me
    just take me.

DRINK to our menfolk, who I think,
    Are most entitled to it,

For if anything drives a gal to drink,
They're the ones to do it.

To mother:

YOU can multiply all the relations of life,
  Have more than one sister or brother,
  In the course of events, have more than one wife,
  But you never can have but one mother.

To women:

DRINK to fair women, who I think,
  Is most entitled to it.
  For if anything drives men to drink,
  They're the ones that do it.

Birthday toasts:

ANOTHER year older? Think this way:
  Just one day older than yesterday.

HAPPY birthday to you, and many to be,
  With friends that are true, as you are to me!

ANOTHER candle on the cake,
  That's no cause to pout,
  Be glad you've still got wind enough
  To blow the damn things out.

TO your birthday, glass held high,
  Glad it's you that's older, not I.

Drinkers' toasts:

THERE'S many a toast, if I could think of it
  Damned if I can, so let's drink to it.

I USED to know a clever toast,
  but damned if I can think of it.
  So raise your glass to anything
  And bugger me, I'll drink to it.

RAISE them high and drink them dry,
  To the bloke who says "My turn to buy."

A GLASS in the hand is worth two on the shelf,
  So tipple it down and refresh yourself.

ONE bottle of beer between the four of us,
  Here's to the luck there's no more of us.

HERE'S to the thirst which is yet to come.

HERE'S to the wowsers, whose abstinence
  gives us all the more to drink.

DRINK and the world drinks with you,
  Swear off, and you drink alone.

DRINK with Impunity. Or anyone else who will share
a glass.

LET'S drink to the soup. May it be seen and not heard.

I DRINK to your health when I'm with you
  I drink to your health when alone
  I drink to your health so often
  I'm becoming concerned at my own.

LET'S drink to the Eskimos' national anthem:
  Freeza jolly good fellow.

AND the Eskimos' toast before sitting down to dinner:
"Whale meet again."

HERE'S to the best thing about a popular song,
and that is that it's not popular too long.

Musicians' toast:

May your organ never quit while you are halfway
through your favourite piece.

Subtle toast:

THE oyster is not the only one to have a crab for a
mate.

Songs

*SONG titles can be well adapted as a toast. The lack
of suitable words shouldn't be an obstacle blocking
the chance for another drink. Just grasp your glass
tightly and quote one of the following:*

DRINK to me only with thine eyes, for I need the
Scotch myself.

HERE'S to the volcano song: Larva come back to me.

I'LL be seizing you, in all the old familiar places.

YOU walrus hurt the one you love.

IF you were the only girl in the world, well okay, but
as you're not, forget it.

I CAN'T get over a girl like you,
  So answer the phone yourself.

SHE used to go with the landlord, but now she goes with the lease.

I USED to kiss her on the lips, but it's all over now.

DON'T sit on the gas stove Granny, you're too old to ride the range.

SHE wore a string of love beads and I knew I could count on her.

AND the Irish chiropractor's patient's song: "My fate is in your hands."

17
Married Life

Marriage

MARRIAGE is a great teacher. It teaches you loyalty, forebearance, self-restraint, meekness, and a great many other qualities you wouldn't need if you had remained single.

ONE good turn gets most of the bedclothes.

IN these times a faithful husband is one whose maintenance payments arrive in time.

A WIFE who drives from the back seat isn't any worse than the husband who cooks from the dining table.

EACH man spoils the one he loves,
    And gratifies her wishes,
    The rich man showers her with gifts,
    The poor man does the dishes.

A WISE man will buy his wife such fine china that she won't trust him to wash the dishes.

A LITTLE woman is a dangerous thing.

LAUGH and the world laughs with you, snore and you sleep alone.

HE said: "Why do you keep reading our marriage certificate?"
  She said: "I'm looking for a loophole."

SHE said one more word and she would go back to her mother. He roared "Taxi!"

A GOOD marriage lasts forever. A bad one just seems to.

I CAN remember where I got married and when I got married, but damned if I can remember why.

MARRIAGE is not a word, it is a sentence.

MARRIAGE is the only life sentence that can be commuted for bad behaviour.

MARRIAGE is not a lottery. In a lottery you have a chance.

MARRIAGE is like a three ring circus. First the engagement ring, second the wedding ring and third the suffer-ring.

MARRIAGE is just another union that defies management.

MARRIAGE is one business that usually has a silent partner.

MARRIAGE is called Holy Acrimony.

MARRIAGES are made uneven.

MARRIAGE these days is a drama in three acts: Announced, Denounced, Renounced.

MARRIAGE is like a violin. When the beautiful music is over the strings are still attached.

THERE'S a lot to be said about marriage. But try not to say it in front of the children.

THE most difficult year of marriage is the one you are in.

MOST marriages are happy. It is trying to live together afterwards that causes the tension.

THE two major causes of marriage break-up are Men and Women.

MONOGAMY leaves a lot to be desired.

REMEMBER, Socrates died from a dose of wedlock.

A CONTENTED husband is one who is on listening terms with his wife.

THE best domestic harmony is when the husband plays second fiddle.

WE have an understanding. One night a week I go out with the boys, and one night a week she does the same thing.

A MATERNITY dress is a magic garment that makes the heir unapparent.

"MARRIED 25 years and your wife looks like a newly-wed?"
   "No. no. I said cooks like a newly-wed."

BEFORE marriage he talks she listens. After marriage she talks he listens. Later they both talk and the neighbours listen.

IF it wasn't for marriage husbands and wives would have to quarrel with strangers.

TWO can live as cheaply as one, and after marriage they do.

BIGAMY is a case of two rites making a wrong.

HE always has the last word in an argument with his wife. It's "yes darling."

AFTER 15 years of marriage they finally achieved sexual compatibility. They both had a headache.

FOR 22 years Harry and his wife were deliriously happy. Then they met each other.

HER husband wears the pants in their house, but she tells him which pair to wear.

MONTY is damned lucky, He has got a wife and a transistor and they both work.

A MAN who thinks he is more intelligent than his wife is married to a very intelligent woman.

GOING to a party with your wife is like going fishing with the game keeper.

"NOW listen," she said as they arrived, "If it's a dull party then let it stay that way."

"TELL me dear, before we were married did you say you were oversexed, or over sex?"

"MONEY, money, money," he said, "they are the only three words you know!"

"I WILL say this for Madge," said the henpecked husband. "Spending money is her only extravagance."

"I'VE been married five years, and believe me, when it comes to making money you've just got to hand it to Madge."

HE said his wife doesn't understand him, but it is his own fault. He shouldn't have married a Chinese girl.

"DOES your wife pick your clothes?"
  "No, only the pockets."

WIFE: "Before we were married you told me you were well off."
  "Yes, but I didn't know it at the time."

THE husband complained: "You never cry out when you have an orgasm."

"How do you know," she replied, "you are never there."

THEY had been married for 15 years. One night while they were making love he said:
"Dear, am I hurting you?"
"No," she replied,"why?"
"I thought you moved," he said.

PADDY was asked how he managed to get along so well with his wife.
"Cos I always tell her the truth, even if I have to lie a little."

MR and Mrs Offenbloo had been married for 20 years and they were still in love. She with the doctor and he with his secretary.

COUNSELLOR: "Are your relations pleasant?"
"Mine are, his are horrible."

"OF course we are incompatible," she said, "but he's far more incompatible than I am."

THE difference between a missus and a mistress is often a mattress.

AS far as our marriage goes there is nothing I wouldn't do for her and nothing she wouldn't do for me. And that's the way it goes, we do nothing for each other.

EVERY woman waits for the right man to come along. But in the meantime, she gets married.

SHE was his secretary before they got married. Now she is his treasurer.

THE man who boasts that he owes everything to his wife should pay her and shut up.

HE was so henpecked he had to wash and iron his own apron.

THE husband took his wife to a marriage counsellor who asked the nature of their problem.

The husband said: "Thingummy here says I don't take enough notice of her."

THEIR marriage is based on trust and understanding.

She doesn't trust him and he doesn't understand her.

HIS mate asked: "Does your wife know you are bringing me home tonight?"

"Oh hell yes. We argued for an hour about it this morning."

"ALRIGHT, so I spend too much money," cried the wife to her nagging husband, "But name just one other extravagance?"

'TIS better to have loved and lost than to have loved and married.

FRED described the bump on his head as a glancing blow.

"The wife caught me glancing at a blonde," he said.

SHE was complaining to her husband. "Why is it taking so long to come up?"

"I'm trying dear, I'm trying," he said. "I just can't think of anyone tonight."

SHE: "How is it that I am always catching you screwing the cook?"

He: "It's because you are always wearing sneakers."

The husband's point of view

NEVER tell your wife that something is as plain as the nose on her face.

A WISE man never laughs at his wife's old clothes.

A HUSBAND is what is left of a lover once the name has been extracted.

A MAN in love is incomplete until he is married. Then he is finished.

UNMARRIED men commit most of the nation's crime, but they are not repeatedly scolded about it.

A BIGAMIST is a man who makes the same mistake twice.

BEFORE criticising your wife's faults, remember that they may have prevented her from getting a better husband.

EVERY married man knows that the most perfect husband in the world belongs to the woman next door.

ONE month after the wedding Arthur began to wonder if he has made the right decision. Every meal had consisted of wedding cake and chips.

THE smart husband thinks twice before saying nothing.

A MAN who says his wife can't take a joke forgets himself.

USUALLY the husband regards himself as the head of the household, and the pedestrian knows he has the right of way. Both of them are safe until they try to prove it.

"I HAVE a clever wife."
  "Mine always finds out, too."

ANYTHING for a quiet wife.

HE said his missus is so determined to have her own way she even writes her diary a month ahead.

A WOMAN doesn't believe a man who says he is unworthy of her, until they are married.

IF your wife doesn't treat you like she should, be thankful.

IF you want your wife to listen, then talk to another woman.

MY wife is a magician. She can turn anything into an argument.

MY wife does bird imitations. She watches me like a hawk.

MY wife has a terrible memory. She never forgets anything.

MY wife always forgives me when she is in the wrong.

MY wife and I started arguing on our wedding day. When I said "I do," she said "Oh no you don't."

MY wife says to me: "Can't we ever have a discussion without you butting in?"

MY wife should get a job in earthquake prediction. She can find a fault quicker than anyone.

THE way my wife finds fault with me you'd think there was a reward.

IT was time to tell the wife who was the boss. So I said: "You're the boss."

THE only males who boss the household are under three years of age.

THE only thing my wife doesn't know is why she married me.

I MET my wife under unfortunate circumstances. I was single.

I TAKE my wife out every night. But she keeps coming back.

I PUT my wife on a pedestal. It makes it easier for her to scrub the ceiling.

I TAKE my wife with me everywhere I go. It's better than kissing her goodbye.

I'VE just got back from a pleasure trip. I've just taken my wife to the airport.

I AM only interested in my wife's happiness. In fact I have hired a private detective to see who is responsible for it.

Funny how a wife can spot a blonde hair on a bloke's coat, yet miss the garage doors

THE only time I find my wife entertaining is when I come home unexpectedly.

SHE accused me of infidelity, but I have been faithful to her lots of times.

SOMETHING terrible has happened. My best friend has run away without my wife.

A HUSBAND? That's a gardener who gets to sleep with the boss of the manor.

"I DIDN'T sleep with my wife before we were married, did you?"
   "I don't know. What was her maiden name?"

THERE'S only one thing that stops me from being happily married, and that's the wife.

WE'VE lost the magic. My wife gave up sex for Lent and I didn't find out until Easter.

"WHAT did you do before you were married?"
   "Anything I wanted to do."

FUNNY how a wife can spot a blonde hair on a bloke's coat, yet miss the garage doors.

HE said he has the kind of wife who spends her evenings dining and whining.

HE hasn't spoken to his wife for a month.
   "I've been unable to interrupt her," he said.

"HAVE you known your wife long?"
"Yes. Ever since we were the same age."

The wife's point of view

BIGAMY is having one husband too many.
Monogomy is the same.

SHE has been married so long she even fakes foreplay.

FIRST she faked chastity, then she faked orgasm and now she fakes fidelity.

IF a woman does household chores for $250 a week, that's domestic science. If she does it for nothing, that's marriage.

EVERY married woman knows that the most considerate wife in the world belongs to the bloke next door.

IN eastern culture a woman never sees her husband before marriage. In western culture she rarely sees him after marriage.

MY husband has a head like a door-knob. Any girl can turn it.

MY husband added some magic to our marriage. He disappeared.

SHE said her husband's average income "was about midnight."

SOME husbands come in handy around the house. Others come in unexpectedly.

NINETY per cent of husbands give the other ten per cent a bad name.

"IS your husband hard to please?"
    "I don't know. I've never tried."

"A HUSBAND like yours is hard to find."
    "He still is."

"DO you cheat on your husband?"
    "Who else?"

THE two women met in the supermarket. "I thought I'd lost 160 kilos of ugly fat. Then Fred came home again."

"FOR months," she said, "I couldn't work out where my husband went every night. Then one night I went home, and there he was."

GIVE a husband enough rope and he'll skip.

MY husband wears the pants, but I tell him which pair to wear.

SHE said she married one of the world's greatest lovers.
    And one day she's going to catch him at it.

Anniversaries

THE most impressive evidence of tolerance is a golden wedding anniversary.

SHE had served him so many burnt offerings that on their first anniversary he bought her an altar cloth.

HE said he couldn't play in the darts team on Saturday.
   "It's our silver wedding anniversary and I've got to take Thingummy out to dinner.

A husband who forgets his wife's anniversary will get something to remember her by.

THE only reason they have stuck together is neither of them will take custody of the kids.

THE biggest surprise you can give your wife on your wedding anniversary is to remember it.

A SILVER anniversary is when two people celebrate the fact that at least 25 years of their marriage is over.

WE'VE been married for 25 years, and I'd like to say that includes five years of wedded bliss.

I ALWAYS remember the wife's birthday. It's the day after she reminds me of it.

ANNIVERSARIES to most men are like toilet seats.
   They invariably miss them.

HE asked how they should celebrate their 25th anniversary.

She suggested two minutes' silence.

AND he reminded everyone that the sentence for manslaughter was only 25 years.

THEY had stuck together so long because neither of them would take custody of the kids.

SHE had been so naive when he married her she thought intercourse was a ticket to the races.

HE said it had been a marriage based on give and take.

He gave, she took.

HIS wife used to have a nice firm chin. But now the firm has taken on a couple of partners.

IT'S no use making your mind up to stay in if your wife has made her face up to go out.

THEY stopped giving each other anniversary presents long ago, now they shake hands each year and call it quits.

Divorce

ONE major reason for divorce is that husbands who promised they would die for their wives, failed to deliver.

NO woman is married to the same man long because he is not the same man long.

ALTHOUGH she divorced him on the grounds that he couldn't consummate the marriage, he had no hard feelings.

THE car salesman divorced his wife. She was giving too many demonstration rides.

HE owed his success to his first wife and his second wife to his success.

BE warned, Monty failed to keep up his maintenance payments and was repossessed by his wife.

SHE was granted a divorce because her husband had flat feet. And they were always in the wrong flat.

SHE said maintenance is the best policy.
   That's a man's cash surrender value.

THEY had to admit she was a great housekeeper.
   Divorced three husbands and kept the house each time.

HE left his wife because of another woman.
   Her mother.

AN Eskimo couple got married at the North Pole. It lasted six months and they called it a day.

THE world's greatest jigsaw player was divorced after his wife found he was keeping a piece on the side.

MY first wife divorced me over a difference of religion. She worshipped money and I didn't have any.

DIVORCES are arranged so that lawyers can live happily ever after.

AFTER she had 13 children she filed for divorce on the grounds of compatibility.

AFTER a Tasmanian divorce do they still call themselves brother and sister?

SHE was very romantic. She insisted on getting divorced in the same dress her mother got divorced in.

MY wife and I are incompatible. I want a divorce and she doesn't.

ONCE upon a time there was a Daddy Bear, a Mummy Bear and a Baby Bear from a previous marriage.

SHE was too meticulous. She divorced me because I had one tiny hair out of place. It was a blonde one on my jacket.

MY wife would divorce me if she could think of a way of doing it without making me happy.

PEOPLE today seem to be marrying more and enjoying it less.

WHEN her divorce came through it made her feel like a new man.

OUR divorce was such an amicable and friendly affair I proposed to her.

Retirement

I ONLY wear the top half of my pyjamas, because I'm semi-retired.

WHEN a man retires and time is no longer of any consequence, his colleagues give him a watch.

RETIREMENT means twice as much husband on half as much money.

ON his retirement the boss told him: "We don't know how we'll replace you; mainly because we still haven't worked out what you did."

AS the boss told him: "As we see it, we're not so much losing a worker as gaining a parking space."

Farewells and funerals

IF you don't go to other people's funerals, they won't go to yours.

THE number of people at your funeral can depend on the weather.

DEATH is nature's way of telling you to slow down.

THE cemeteries are full of people who thought the world couldn't get along without them.

HAVE you noticed how everybody dies in alphabetical order each day?

UNDERTAKERS have raised the cost of funerals by 20% due to the high cost of living.

THE man who said "you can't take it with you," no doubt had the cost of funerals in mind.

HER husband didn't leave her much when he died. But he left her a lot while he was living.

YOU should never say anything about the dead unless it's good. Like, "He's dead, and that's good."

ALL my uncle left was a grandfather clock, so there wasn't much trouble winding up his estate.

"WHAT'S the death rate in this town?"
   "Same as anywhere. One per person."

THE wife said she had been thinking things over and that she had finally decided she wanted to be cremated.
   "Okay," he said, "Get yer coat on."

GRANDFATHER'S funeral has cost 50 dollars. We buried him in a rented suit.

HIS will was one of the shortest. It said: "Being of sound mind I spent all my money."

MY sister is going out with an undertaker. We suspect he only wants her for her body.

THE difference between a funeral and a wedding is one less drunk.

THE cemeteries are full of people who thought the world couldn't get along without them.

UNCLE Fred died of asbestosis. It took three weeks to cremate the old bugger.

TO Death, that jolly old reaper now,
    Let our glasses be a clinking,
    If he hadn't called old John, I vow,
    Tonight we'd not be drinking.

ON an old maid's tombstone: "Who said you can't take it with you?"

SHE had been such a good time girl all her life they had to bury her in a Y-shaped coffin.

AND the epitaph on her tombstone read: "At last she sleeps alone."

SHE said that when her sugar daddy dies she inherits the lot. "It's in his will and testicles."
    "You mean testament."
    "No," she said, "I've got him by the balls."

18
Miscellaneous Advice

Advice, good and bad

GIVE neither counsel nor salt unless asked for it. *Old Proverb.*

ADVICE is a dangerous gift; be cautious about giving and receiving it.

ADVICE is what we ask for when we already know the answer and wish we didn't.

IF you can distinguish between good advice and bad advice, then you don't need advice.

TRUST only those who stand to lose as much as you if things go wrong.

TRUST everybody, but insist on shuffling the cards.

A GOOD shock is worth more to a man than good advice.

YOU will never hit your thumb with a hammer if you hold the hammer with both hands.

ADVICE is seldom welcome, and those who need it most like it least.

NEVER fart in a lift unless you are sure of getting out at the next floor.

NEVER ever suffer in silence.

ALWAYS remember your lies.

ALWAYS be the one to start rumours, otherwise you won't know if they're true.

IF at first you don't succeed, destroy all evidence that you tried.

IT is worth scheming to be the bearer of good news, and absent when bad news is expected.

NEVER ask a barber if you need a haircut.

NEVER do card tricks for the group you play poker with.

NEVER argue with a woman when she is tired - or rested.

NEVER leave a turn unstoned.

NEVER put off till tomorrow what you can avoid altogether.

NEVER go round with another man's wife, unless you can go a round with her husband.

NEVER stand between a tree stump and a dog.

NEVER kiss at the garden gate,
  love is blind, but the neighbours aint.

NEVER be first, never be last, never volunteer for anything.

NEVER walk through the office without a piece of paper in your hand.

NEVER do anything you wouldn't be caught dead doing.

NEVER try to pacify someone at the height of their rage.

NEVER take the blonde secretary out for coffee. It's too hard to retrain her.

NEVER take whisky without water, and never take water without whisky.

ALWAYS say no, then negotiate.

ALWAYS hire a rich lawyer.

NEVER buy from a rich salesman.

WHATEVER happens, look as though it was intended.

KNICKERLESS girls should never climb trees.

DON'T take moderation to extremes.

AVOID cliches like the plague.

AVOID wet dreams. Sell your water bed.

AVOID hangovers. Stay drunk.

IF we can't be honest with each other, let's lie together.

EAT prunes and get a good run for your money.

GIVE orthopaedic surgeons a break.

SMOKING takes years off your life. So smoke and stay younger.

ADVICE for worms: Sleep Late!

KNOCK firmly, but softly. The world needs soft, firm knockers.

CUT out the middle man. Shit in the river.

DON'T be ashamed of your police record. Have the courage of your convictions.

PEOPLE who love sausages and respect the law should never watch either being made.

THE only time to be positive is when you are certain you are wrong.

WHEN packing for holidays take half as much clothing and twice as much money.

DON'T put all your bags in one exit.

IF you see an unattended bag, go up and talk to her.

A WORD of advice: Don't give it.

Questions without answers

DROP the odd question on your listeners from time to time. It prods them to participate. Don't expect an answer for there are none, but at least they will be impressed by the depth and profundity of these esoteric queries.

WHICH of us is the opposite sex?

WHAT has posterity ever done for me?

WHY isn't phonetic spelled the way it sounds?

WHY is abbreviation such a long word?

WHY is it that wrong numbers are never out when you call?

HAVE you ever imagined a world with no hypothetical situations?

IF ignorance is bliss, why do we have school exams?

WAS Handel a crank?

IF Maggie's hair falls out will we have to re-Thatcher?

IF the world is getting smaller, why are telephone bills getting bigger?

WHY do women say they have been shopping when they haven't bought anything?

WHY do big women turn into little old ladies?

WHY do you need a driver's licence to buy liquor when you can't drink and drive?

WHY do we drive on parkways and park on driveways?

WHY is it that something sent by car is a shipment and something sent by ship is a cargo?

HOW do mosquitos get along without sleep?

CAN a self-made man pull himself to pieces?

COULD a half-wit work part-time for Intelligence?

IF men wear jock straps, do women wear fan belts?

DO you need a silencer if you are going to shoot a mime?

IF you tied buttered toast to the back of a cat and dropped it from a height, what would happen?

WHAT is the probability that something will happen according to the odds?

WHAT did we do before we discovered nostalgia?

IF I like sadism, necrophilia and bestiality,
   do you think I'm flogging a dead horse?

IF you are in a vehicle going at the speed of light,
   what happens when you turn on the headlights?

WHO is General Failure and why is he reading my disk?

WAS King Kong the original urban gorilla?

IF the little black box on aircraft is indestructible why don't they make the whole bloody plane out of the same stuff?

WHY is it that when you are driving and looking for an address you turn down the volume on the radio?

IS Johnny Cash change from a condom vending machine?

WHY don't you buy 144 condoms and be grossly oversexed?

IS a tom-tit a transvestite's falsie?

IS a lesbian a pansy without a stalk?

IS camping loitering within tent?

IS Red Riding Hood a Russian contraceptive?

IS a castrated pig disgruntled?

DOES the lateral coital position mean having a bit on the side?

SHOULD single crabs have nippers?

CAN a cross-eyed teacher control her pupils?

IS it cruel to sew buttons on flies?

IS the real Jewish dilemma Free Pork?

IF the world's wizards, magicians, and witchdoctors all arrived on the same plane would that be a Mumbo Jumbo?

IF a light sleeper sleeps with the light on, does a hard sleeper sleep with the window open?

DO fur covered toilet seats tickle your fancy?

IS a lady barrister without briefs a solicitor?

COULD a drinking lizard be any flatter?

IS the Pope's wife a Catholic?

DO bears shit in the woods?

INSTEAD of having ballet girls prancing around on tiptoe why don't they hire taller dancers?

IF the world is getting smaller why do they keep raising postal rates?

IF necessity is the mother of invention, how come so much unnecessary junk gets invented?

WHY do they call it "take home pay" when it should be called "left-overs?"

HOW do chooks know the size of our egg cups?

WHY doesn't idle rumour remain idle?

HAVE you noticed how people die in alphabetical order?

WHY is it that wrong phone numbers are never busy.

WHAT good are rhetorical questions?

"WELL, if I rang the wrong number, why did you answer the phone?"

Questions with answers

WHAT'S got 50 balls, is 5 centimetres long and fucks ducks?
   A shotgun cartridge.

WHY do rabbis always answer a question with another question?
   Why not?

WHAT does an Aborigine call a boomerang that doesn't come back?
   A stick.

WHAT'S got 75 balls and screws old ladies?
   Bingo.

WHY do dogs lick their balls?
  Because they can.

WHAT has four legs and flies?
  A dead horse!

WHAT'S grey and comes in buckets?
  An elephant.

WHAT do husbands have in their pants that their wives
don't want on their faces?
  Wrinkles.

WHAT is pink and wrinkly and hangs out your pants?
  Your grandma.

WHY has an elephant got four feet?
  Because he would look silly with six inches.

WHY do so many brides start to get crow's feet as
soon as they are married?
  From squinting and saying: "Is that as big as it
gets?"

WHAT'S six inches long, has a bald head and drives
Jewish women wild?
  An American hundred dollar note.

WHAT does it take to circumcise a whale?
  Fore skin divers.

WHY don't rabbits make a noise when they root?
  Because they have cotton balls.

WHY is a joke like a pussy?
  Neither is any good if you don't get it.

WHAT do light and hard have in common?
  You can't sleep with a light on either.

WHAT'S black and white and eats like a horse?
  A Zebra.

WHY are pubic hairs curly?
  So they don't poke your eyes out.

HOW do you stop a woman giving you head?
  Marry her.

WHAT'S better than a bird in the hand?
  A hand in the bush.

WHAT do Christmas trees and vasectomised men have in common?
  They both have balls for decoration.

HOW can you tell the sex of a chromosome?
  Take down its genes.

HOW can you tell if pancakes are male or female?
  Female pancakes are well stacked.

QUESTION: How many car salesmen does it take to change a light bulb?
  Answer: "Take a seat sir. I'll work it out on my calculator and you will be very pleasantly surprised."

WHAT do you get when cross a Jehovah's Witness with a Bikie?

Somebody who knocks on your door and tells YOU to Piss Off!"

WHY do heretics scrawl the message: "Fuck the Pope?"

Because normally there is neither the time nor the chalk to write "Fuck the Moderator of the General Synod of the Presbyterian Assembly."

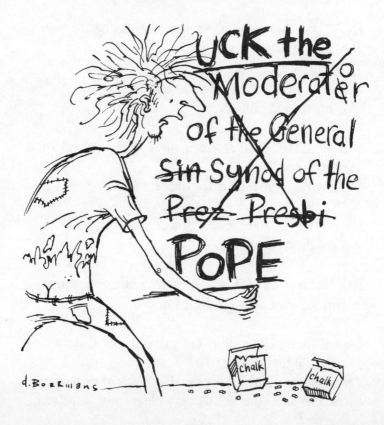

Differences

WHAT'S the difference between erotic and kinky?
    Erotic is when you use a feather.
    Kinky is when you use the whole chicken.

WHAT'S the difference between a vitamin and a hormone?
    You can't hear a vitamin.

WHAT'S the difference between a condom and a pork pie?
    You get more meat in a condom.

WHAT'S the difference between a milk-maid and a stripper?
    The milk-maid is fair and buxom ...

WHAT'S the difference between a slut and a bitch?
    A slut will sleep with anyone.
A bitch will sleep with anyone, but you.

THE difference between a vacuum cleaner and a randy Swiss admiral is that one sucks and never fails, and the other gets seasick.

THE difference between a virgin and a light bulb is, you can't unscrew a light bulb.

THE difference between a smart blonde and the Loch Ness Monster is that there are some people who think the monster exists.

THE difference between a brick and a blonde is that one of them doesn't follow you around for weeks after you've laid it.

THE difference between a clitoris and a golf ball is that some blokes can spend 30 minutes looking for a golf ball.

THE difference between beer nuts and deer nuts is that one is about $2 a packet and the other is under a buck.

WHAT'S the difference between a woman in church and a woman in the bath?
    One has a soul full of hope ...

THE difference between a blonde and a computer is only discovered when they go down on you.

THE difference between a monkey and a hooker is that one lies on its back for peanuts while the other lives at the zoo.

THE difference between a pothole and a politician is that you would swerve to avoid the pothole.

THE difference between a knight and a baker is that one darts into the foe, while the other makes bread.

THE difference between a cavalry horse and a draught horse is that one darts into the fray and the other works for the council.

THE difference between a mountain goat and a gold fish is that one mucks about the fountain and the other climbs steep hills.

THE difference between a thin prostitute and a counterfeit note is that one is a phoney buck ...

THE difference between unlawful and illegal is that one is against the law and the other is a sick bird.

THE difference between a rooster and a lawyer is that the rooster clucks defiance ...

THE difference between a magician's wand and a policeman's baton is that one is for cunning stunts ...

Dabbler's dictionary

ABILITY: What you need if the boss has no daughter.

ABSENTEE: A missing golfing accessory.

ABUNDANCE: A local hop usually staged in a barn.

ACME: Pimples on the face running towards the top.

ADAM: The first white slave.

ADAMANT: The very first insect.

ADIEU: Hymie Finklestein.

ADOLESCENCE: When a girl's voice changes from No to Yes.

ADORN: What comes after the darkest hour.

ADVERTISEMENT: Something that makes you think you've longed for it for years, but never heard of it before.

AETIOLOGY: A lost cause.

ALIMONY: A mistake by two people paid for by one.

ALPHABET: Not quite the complete wager.

AMNESIA: Best forgotten.

ANTI-CLIMAX: Bore-gasm.

ANTI-DISESTABLISHMENTARIANISM: Easier done than said.

ANTI-FREEZE: When you don't talk to your uncle's wife.

ANXIETY: Nothing to worry about.

APATHY: Not worth worrying about.

APEX: The female of the gorilla species.

ARCHEOLOGIST: A man whose career lies in ruins.

AROMATIC: An automatic longbow.

ARTFUL: A painting gallery.

ASTRONAUT: One who is glad to be down and out.

AUTOBIOGRAPHY: The car's logbook.

AUTOMATIC SHIFT: Driver moving closer to his girlfriend.

AUTOPSY: A dying practice.

AVAIL: Helpful for ugly women.

AVERAGE: Poorest of the good and best of the bad.

AWE-STRUCK: Being hit with a paddle.

BACHELOR: A bloke who never finds out how many faults he has.

BACTERIA: A modern self-service TAB.

BADMINTON: The reason the lamb tasted off.

BALANCE: Something you lose if the bank pushes you.

BARBARIAN: The bloke who cuts your hair.

BARGAIN: Something you figure out a use for once you've bought it.

BATHING SUIT: A garment cut to see level.

BESTIALITY: A pig in a poke.

BIGAMIST: A fog over Italy.

BIGOTRY: Being married to two or more people.

BIGOTRY: An Italian redwood.

BLACK EYE: A stamp of disapproval.

BLUNDERBUSS: A coach which goes from Melbourne to Sydney, via Port Augusta.

BOOKCASE: Litigation about a novel which ensures wide sales.

BORE: A bloke who, when you ask him how he is, tells you.

BORN EXECUTIVE: A bloke whose father owns the company.

BOXER: A bloke who stands up for the other fellow's rights.

BRAZIER: Something to warm your hands on.

BRUSSELS SPROUT: A famous statue found in that city.

BURLESQUE SHOW: Where attendance falls off if nothing else does.

CABBAGE: The fare you pay a taxi driver.

CHILDBIRTH: The fruits of your labour.

CLIMATE: The best thing to do with a ladder.

CLOAK: The mating call of a Chinese frog.

CONDOM: A sock in the puss.

CONDOM: An item to be worn on every conceivable occasion.

CONDOMS: Homes for retired semen.

CONSCIENCE: The ache when everything else feels good.

CONTRACEPTION: Avoiding the issue.

COPULATE: What an Italian police chief says to an officer who doesn't get to work on time.

CORPORATE VIRGIN: New girl in the office.

COWARD: A man who thinks with his legs.

CUNNILINGUS: A real tongue twister.

CYNIC: One who looks down his nose on those above.

DEPRESSIVE NEUROSIS: Nothing to laugh about.

DESPERATE STRAIGHTS: Sex-starved heterosexuals.

DETEST: The West Indies playing India.

DIAPHRAMS: Trampolines for dickheads.

DIPLOMACY: Letting someone else have your way.

DUCK DICK: A game warden.

ECSTACY: It's the feeling you feel when you feel you are going to feel a feeling you have never felt before.

ELECTRICIAN: A switch doctor.

ENGLISH GENT: One who gets out of the bath to piss in the sink.

EUNUCH: Massive vassel with a passive tassel.

EXCEPTIONS: Always outnumber rules.

EXPERIENCE: What we call our mistakes.

EXTREME UNCTION: The last word.

FASTIDIOUS: A girl who is fast and hideous.

FAUCET: What you have to do if the tap won't turn.

FELLATIO: The French connection.

FERTILIZERS: A growth industry.

FETE: A boring picnic worse than death.

FLOOZIE: A sweet girl with the gift of the grab.

GAELIC: An Irish lesbian.

GALLERY: A hostel for young women.

GAY MILKMAN: Dairy queen.

GENITALIA: Not an Italian airline.

GENITALS: Non-Jewish.

GERIATRIC: A German cricketer who takes three wickets.

GLUTTON: The bloke who takes the cake you wanted.

GOSSIP: Letting the chat out of the bag.

GRANARY: A home for senior female citizens.

GRAVITY is starting to get me down.

HALITOSIS: Better than no breath at all.

HEBREW: a male teabag.

HEN'S PARTY: A bunch of birds cackling about who is laying whom.

HIGH FIDELITY: A drunk who always goes home to his wife.

HORIZON: Callgirl getting up in the morning.

HORS-D'OEUVRE: A ham sandwich cut in 50 pieces.

HUMBUG: A singing cockroach.

HUMMINGBIRDS: Parrots that have forgotten the words.

HYACINTH: A yank greeting a gal called Cynthia.

IDOLISE: Eyes that refuse to look at anything.

INCEST: Rolling your own.

INCEST: Relatively boring.

INCOME: What you have to make first, because you can't make it last.

INDECISION: The key to flexibility.

INNUENDO: An Italian suppository.

INSOMNIA: Nothing to lose sleep over.

IRISH PILLION PASSENGER: Pat on the back.

JEALOUSY: The friendship one woman shares with another.

JEWISH DILEMMA: Free pork.

LACTIC: A grandfather clock which doesn't work.

LESBIAN COCKTAIL LOUNGE: Her-She bar.

LESBIAN: A manic depressive with illusions of gender.

LESBIANS: Insurmountable odds.

LETTER-BOMBS: Post mortems.

LIBERAL: A Conservative who's been arrested.

LIFE: A Sexually-transmitted terminal disease.

LISTENING: Silent flattery.

LUBRICATED CONDOMS: Bedroom slippers.

MADAM: One who offers vice to the lovelorn.

MARCONI: The first man to send a message through a length of spaghetti without touching the sides.

MASTURBATION: I-balling.

MATURITY: For those who've decided to grow old.

MILITARY INTELLIGENCE: A contradiction in terms.

MINE SHAFT: What a German calls his dick.

MONOGOMY: Leaves a lot to be desired.

MONOLOGUE: A discussion between man and wife.

NIHILISM: Bound to come to nothing.

NONEDESCRIPT: A television play.

NOSTALGIA: Not what it used to be.

NUMERACY: Doesn't count these days.

OBESITY: Surplus gone to waist.

ODIOUS: Not very good poetry.

ORGASMS: Usually an anti-climax.

ORGY: Grope therapy.

PARACHUTING: Jumping to conclusions.

PARASITE: Somebody who lives in Paris.

PARENTS: Couples who practice the Rythym Method.

PEDESTRIAN: A motorist with teenage sons.

PERFORATIONS: Usually a rip-off.

PIECE DE RESISTANCE: A French virgin.

PIMP: Nookie Bookie.

PIMP: Public relations man for a public relations girl.

PORNOGRAPHY: One-handed literature.

PORNOGRAPHY: Cliterature.

POSSIBLY: Three syllables meaning either yes or no.

PRAISE: Something received when you are no longer alive.

PREDESTINATION: Doomed from the start.

PREMATURE EJACULATION: The come before the scorn.

PSEUDONYM: A nym that's not your real nym.

RACIAL DISPUTE: When the course judge calls for a photo.

RED RIDING HOOD: A Russian condom.

REFLECTION: What a girl looks at, but is not given to.

SAGE: A bloke who knows his onions.

SELF-DECEPTION: Faking an organism during masturbation.

SHINS: For finding furniture in the dark.

SITTING PRETTY: Sitting Bull's gay brother.

SNOW JOB: How a woman defrosts her man.

SNUFF: Sufficient unto the day.

SOLITUDE: Best when shared with someone.

SONATA: A song sung by Frank.

SPECIMEN: An Italian astronaut.

STALEMATE: A husband who has lost his ardour.

SUICIDE: The sincerest form of self-criticism.

SUNGLASSES: Optical seclusion.

TACT: The ability to describe others as they see themselves.

TEAR JERKER: A bloke who cries while wanking.

TRANSVESTITES: Skirting the issue.

TRUE LOVE: An injection with affection to the mid-section from a projection without objection.

TUTANKHAMEN: Mummy's boy.

UNEMPLOYMENT: The new growth industry.

URETHRA: Not a famous black gospel singer.

VICE SQUAD: The pussy posse.

VICE VERSA: Dirty poetry from Italy.

VIRGIN SQUAW: Wouldn't Indian.

VIRGIN: A girl who whispers sweet nothing doings.

VIRGIN: A girl who won't take in what a guy takes out.

VIRGIN: Any Hicksville girl who can outrun her brothers.

VULGARITY: The conduct of others.

WELSH RAREBIT: A Cardiff virgin.

WET DREAM: A snorgasm.

News reports

IF you really want an excuse to interrupt yourself during a speech why not hand yourself a news report? It gives you a legitimate excuse to read them because they are supposed to be news to you too.

POLICE investigations now reveal that the skeleton discovered under the floorboards of the Launceston Hotel was that of the Tasmanian Hide & Seek Champion.

NEWS Flash! A helicopter crashed into the cemetery of an Irish village this afternoon. At last count 705 bodies had been recovered.

IT has just been reported that the City of Glasgow has recently raised public transport fares so that the citizens can increase their savings by walking.

THE Baptist synod has just banned stand up sex. The synod believes it could well lead to dancing.

I HAVE just been informed that this is the time of year when policemen and firemen hold their balls.

EASTER has been cancelled. They've found the body.

CHRISTMAS has been cancelled. They've found the father.

DOLLY Parton has just had a single come out.

THEY have just invented a contraceptive pill for men. It is a little pebble that you put in your shoe and it makes you limp.

THERE is a health crisis in Zanzibar where the witch-doctors have made a world-wide appeal for leeches. The Australian government has responded by sending a plane load of real estate agents.

A MAN arrested for putting German coins in a parking meter pleaded not guilty because his car was a Volkswagen.

AT a city hotel a waiter was dismissed for having his thumb in the soup and a topless waitress was dismissed for two similar offences.

DUTCH Realms disease has just been reported in the Royal family of Holland.

Crossings

IF you cross a homing pigeon with a parrot you get a bird that asks the way home when it gets lost.

IF you cross a parrot with a centipede you get a walkie-talkie.

IF you cross a road with a chicken you'll get the answer we've all been looking for.

IF you cross a bridge with a car you'll get to the other side.

NEVER cross a disobedient dog with a rooster.
   You will only get a cock that doesn't come.

BETTER to cross a rooster with an owl,
   and get a cock that stays up all night.

HE once crossed a field with Mary Poppins and got nothing.

Signs of the times

A journalist always has the advantage of having a notebook in the pocket to capture the many quirky signs that can tickle the fancy. Here are a few spells of bad English collected in this manner from both home and abroad:

CUSTOMERS who pay for their meals then leave without eating will be prosecuted.

TRY our pies. You'll never get better.

BUY "Woof" the pet food dogs ask for by name.

THE water in this establishment has been personally passed by the proprietor.

SIGN outside an optician's: If you don't see what you want you have come to the right place.

SIGN outside a dry cleaner's: Drop your dacks here!

PLAYERS picked for the darts team will be pinned on the notice board.

SIGN at the beauty parlour: Don't whistle at the girl leaving here. She may be your grandmother.

SIGN at pawnbroker's: See me at your earliest inconvenience.

SIGN on a bankrupt retail store: Opened by mistake.

IN several pubs: We have an agreement with the bank. They don't serve beer and we don't cash cheques.

IN a Scottish pub: Happy Hour 5.30pm until 6pm.

LADIES are requested not to have children in the bar.

LOST & Found ad: To the party that shot an arrow in the air and knows not where. Contact Room 502, General Hospital.

DON'T drink if you're driving. There's no cure for the mourning after.

IF you are driving be sure you have a car.

DON'T drive yourself to drink. Get a chauffeur.

ONE for the road could be the pint of no return.

PLEASE do not leave while the bar is in motion.

THIRST come, thirst served.

OUTSIDE the Registry Office: Marry now. Pay later.

SIGN outside the church: Next week's preacher will be pinned on the Notice Board.

DIRECTIONS on a jam jar: To open lid, pierce with knife to release vacuum, then push off.

PATRONS who consider our staff uncivil should see the manager. *New Delhi restaurant.*

CUSTOMERS giving orders will be promptly executed. *New Delhi restaurant.*

PATRONS who require bathing, please notice the chambermaid. *German Hotel.*

IN case of fire, please do your best to alarm the porter.

TO avoid burning your hands with hot water, feel the water first before putting your hands in.

INSTANT hot water, in two minutes.

TOILETS out of order. Please use Platforms 7 and 8.

SIGN in a fruit shop: God help those who help themselves.

SIGN in a bookshop: Browsers welcome, both high browse and low browse.

SIGN in returned servicemen's club: Don't thump the machines, look for an attendant.

THE all-night Chinese take-away is called Wok Around the Clock.

ENGLISH sign in Swiss hotel: If you have any desires during the night, please ring the receptionist.

BOAT for sale, one owner, green in colour.

OUT to lunch. If not back by five, out to dinner also.

SIGN outside funeral parlour: Parking for clients only.

WANTED. Man to wash dishes and two waitresses.

PRICES subject to change according to customer's attitude.

SIGN at a creek: When this sign is underwater a crossing is dangerous.

SIGN in a pub: If you are drinking to forget, please pay for your drinks in advance.

PLEASE do not insult our bartenders. Customers we can get.

ON the front door of a travel agency: Go away!

OUTSIDE butcher shop: Nobody can beat our meat!

FINANCIER'S brochure: Now you can borrow enough money to get completely out of debt.

SINGAPORE Hotel: Do not use the diving board when swimming pool is empty.

CHOICE of the day in a Beirut hotel restaurant: We highly recommend the hotel tart.

IN a Cairo elevator: Keep your hands away from unnecessary buttons.

PLEASE hang your order before retiring on the doorknob.

TO call room service, just open the door and call room service.

SPORTS jackets must be worn in the dining room. Trousers are optional.

DANCE to music while you overlook a fascinating view of the the beach.

AT a Cairo zoo. Please don't feed the animals. If you have any spare food hand it to the attendants.

IN an Indian maternity hospital: Visitors. Husbands only. One per patient.

EARS pierced while you wait.

ON an Irish shop: Gone to lunch, back in an hour. PS: Already gone 15 minutes.

GOOD clean entertainment every night except Monday.

Advertisements

LOST dog. Has three legs, blind in one eye. Right ear missing, broken tail, no teeth, recently castrated. Answers to Lucky.

ADVERTISEMENT in local newspaper: Editor urgently needs poof reader.

CLASSIFIED ad: Used gravestone for sale. Ideal gift for family called McTavish.

FOR sale: Bulldog. Eats anything. Loves children.

FOR sale: Ten-volt smoke alarm, with silencer.

GIRL wanted for petrol pump attendant.

BI-SEXUAL man, aged 40, seeks married couple.

EXTREMELY independent male needs to rent room. Call mother on 580-6683.

AVAILABLE. French secretary who speaks floorless English.

BUY six and get two!

PLACED in the personal column: Fred, do not come home, all is forgiven.

ACCOMMODATION: Suit two girls willing to share room, or young man.

ACCOMMODATION: Honeymoon suite, sleeps three.

STRADIVARIUS violin for sale. Almost new.

Showbiz, musicians and theatre

CALL yourself a comedian? Don't make me laugh.

THE new musical was so bad a bloke asked a lady sitting in front of him to put her hat on.

YOU can always tell how bad a musical is by the number of times the chorus yell "Encore!"

AN actor believes that a small role is better than a long loaf.

IF Mozart was alive today he would be celebrating the 150th anniversary of his death.

STRADIVARIUS sold his violins on the open market with no strings attached.

BEETHOVEN was so deaf he thought he was a painter.

A TRUE music lover is the man who puts his ear to the keyhole when he hears a woman singing in the bath.

A TRUE music lover is the woman who applauds when her husband comes home singing at dawn.

UNCLE Fred is a musician. He goes out every night fit as a fiddle and comes home tight as a drum.

AT one time singers used to require musicians to accompany them. Since the advent of synthesisers singers can now play with themselves.

SINCE she played Lot's wife she has never looked back.

MANY a starlet trying to make it to the top often wears clothes that don't.

GIRLS are like pianos. When they are not upright, they're grand.

I PLAY the piano like Mozart, with both hands.

I PLAY in a very small quartet. There are only three of us.

IN the orchestra he plays piano. At home he plays second fiddle.

MY brother was known as the Van Gogh of the violin. He had no ear for it.

My sister used to play the banjo until she married. Now she picks on her husband.

HE is an original player. He makes a lot of mistakes, but they are always different each time.

A STAR is a person who pays his publicist a fabulous fee to get famous, then wears dark glasses to avoid being recognised.

HE didn't have $50 to see the Broadway musical, Cats, so he settled for some off-Broadway pussy for $25.

SHE was a big star now, but originally she was the good time had by all.

ON receiving the Oscar the actor said: "I don't deserve this honour. But on the other hand, I've got arthritis and I don't deserve that either."

AN earnest young man with a violin case under his arm asked the London bobby: "How do I get to Albert Hall?"
    "Practice, practice, practice," said the cop.

THE old lady asked the busker, "Do you always play by ear?"
    "No, missus, sometimes I play over there."

PADDY Murphy thought the Guinness Book of Records was an LP of Irish drinking songs.

I AM writing a drinking song, but I can't get past the first few bars.

HE was a short-sighted musician and one day fell over a clef.

SHE went out with a musician once and hasn't been composed since.

I CAN'T sing, so I'm looking for a ravishing blonde accompanist who can't play the piano.

HE used to be married to a trapeze artist, but she caught him in the act.

SHE danced ballet with her left leg and tap with her right and between them she made a fortune.

MALE porno stars get it easy.
   They can get away with muffing their lines.

DANCING is the perpendicular expression of horizontal desire.

DANCING is a physical contact sport.

I DON'T dance, but I'd like to hold you while you do.

THE contralto had a large repertoire, and her tight dress showed it off to advantage.

AND now we have Miss Lottza Bazooma to perform the Dance of the Virgin, entirely from memory.

AFTER listening to the maestro play a piano concerto the adoring fan said: "I'd give my right arm to play like that."

AN AGENT is somebody who thinks a performer is a person who takes 90 per cent of his money from him.

A CELEBRITY is simply an actor who has a publicity agent.

MY agent said with a face like mine I should be in radio.

WHEN is an actor not an actor?
Most of the time.

THE film was so bad we had to sit through it three times to get our money's worth.

IN the Hollywood set if you don't have your own psychiatrist, people think you are crazy.

THERE is a new Israeli group called the Fore Skins.
They are backed by Jock Strap and his Elastic Band playing "Stop that Swing."

Sales and salesmen

So many conventions revolve around motivation for sales campaigns that it is opportune for the speaker to hit his listeners with a few sharp pointers on salesmanship.

WHEN you knock on her door and her husband opens it...Sell something. For Chris'sake sell something.

AS the shoe salesman said: "Can I interest you in a casual pump?"
She said: "Why not? I can look at the footwear later."

THE car salesman divorced his wife.
She was giving too many demonstration rides.

"THERE'S a salesman outside with a young lady."
   "Tell him I'll take one."

TWO pros met on the street. "How's business?" said one.
   "Slim prickings," said the other.

TAKE the Real Estate Agent's advice: Get Lots While You Can.

SALES resistance, of course, is the triumph of mind over patter.

"HOW did the new salesman go today?"
   "He got two orders. One to get out, and one to stay out."

FROM the For Sale section of the newspaper: Home Computer, as new. Never been figured out.

A HIGH-PRESSURE car salesman told his client. "Do you realise that while you are standing here dithering your car is depreciating?"

EARRING special for pirates. Only a buck-an-ear.

MINI-tampons on sale. For short period only.

Fashions

KEEPING up with the fashions means in one era and out the other.

THE only fashion statement her clothes made were "No comment."

HE told his wife she should wear her dresses longer; about three years longer.

NOTHING can replace the old-fashioned cover-all swim suit, and it practically has.

THE wife has two wardrobes jam-packed with nothing to wear.

SHE looked as though she just threw something on, and missed.

SHE looked as though she was poured into her dress and forgot to say when.

SHE was wearing one of those dresses that holds on tight going around curves.

IT'S not the cost of a strapless gown, it's the upkeep.

THE debutante wore a beautiful gownless evening strap.

HER dress looked pretty good considering the shape it was on.

THE outfit made her look like a million dollars, all wrinkled and green.

A TIGHT skirt has never yet stopped a girl's circulation.

THE latest thing in women's clothing is men.

ACCORDING to the latest fashion magazine, women will be wearing their legs longer this summer.

WHEN he heard that French women would not be wearing dresses much longer this season he decided to go there for his holidays.

HE asked what Mabel's new dress looked like.
　He was told that in a lot of places it looks like Mabel.

"LOOK at this bargain?" she told her husband, "I bought it for a ridiculous figure."
　"Yeah, but how much did you pay for it?"

"WHENEVER I am down in the dumps I treat myself to a new hat."
　"We wondered where you got them."

Statistics

WE can all make wonderous statements using statistics which never fail to impress the listener. They can prove anything, even the truth.

STATISTICS prove that 50% of all people who get married at Easter are women.

STATISTICS prove that 25% of accidents were caused by drunk drivers. Which means that the other 75% were caused by non-drinkers.

ON the question why men liked girls legs, 19% said they liked fat legs, 27% said they liked slender legs and the rest said they liked something in between.

95% of all motorists consider themselves to be above average drivers.

80% of bishops take The Times. The other 20% buy it.

STATISTICS prove that average intelligence is being less stupid than half the people and more stupid than the other half.

CIGARETTES are by far the major cause of statistics.

TWO people in every one is a schizophrenic.

STATISTICS prove that the best time to visit Paris is between your 18th and 25th birthdays.

WHEN O'Reilly read that 70 per cent of accidents happen within a mile of home, he moved.

LATEST surveys prove you cannot produce a baby in one month by impregnating nine women.

90% of the population have been caused by accident.

BEDS cause hangovers. Statistics prove that drunks will go to bed happy, and wake up feeling terrible.

SURVEYS show there are seven million fat people in Australia, in round figures.

THE latest statistics indicate that the best time to buy anything was a year ago.

SURVEYS show there are more deaf people engaged in writing popular songs than in any other occupation.

NOTHING can be so deceptive as statistics, except figures.

STATISTICS are like lawyers. They will testify for either side.

SOME day an enterprising statistician will figure out the time lost in compiling statistics.